CONTENTS

KU-637-213

WINDOW GARDENS

Lizzie Boyd

PELHAM BOOKS
LONDON

First published in Great Britain by
Pelham Books Ltd
44 Bedford Square
London WC1B 3DP
1985

Designed and produced by
The Rainbird Publishing Group Ltd
40 Park Street, London W1Y 4DE

House editor: Jasmine Taylor
Designer: Roy Williams
Picture researcher: Celia Dearing

British Library Cataloguing in Publication Data
Boyd, Lizzie
    Window gardens.
    1. Window-gardening
    I. Title
    635.9′65   SB419

ISBN 0-7207-1560-1

Text set by Bookworm Typesetting,
Manchester, England
Illustrations originated by Anglia Reproductions,
Witham, Essex, England
Printed and bound by Printer Industria Gràfica
SA, Barcelona, Spain D.L.B 37454 – 1984

WINDOW
GARDENS

INTRODUCTION

Window gardening does not begin and end with window boxes: it extends to the whole façade of a house. As with skilfully applied make-up, window dressing can highlight a prominent feature or, perhaps, play down a blemish.

Windows are the 'eyes' of a house, expressing its personality and offering a cheerful welcome. They may be painted with bright colours or quiet elegance, but the true flair in window gardening lies in assessing the character of the house, matching, for example, rustic charm with oldtime flower favourites, or the stylish town look with elegant plants of architectural shape. Narrow ledges and huge picture windows, tiny embrasures and large balconies, dark basements and sundrenched courtyards are all potentially rich and often under-utilized areas that offer immense scope for decorating with plants. And not only from the outside – greenery and brilliant blooms, warm behind the glass, are equally important for the well-dressed window.

Large expanses of bare house walls can be clothed with shrubs and climbers forming living 'curtains', while on a smaller scale wall containers and half-baskets can spill over with equally charming draperies. Containers and pots of all shapes and sizes can replace traditional beds of soil and become homes for permanent and temporary plants, following the changing seasons so that even in the depth of winter, life and colour are never absent. The numerous colour illustrations in this book are an inspiration and show just what can be achieved with a little imagination.

Window gardening is almost pure pleasure, for it involves neither hard work nor heavy financial outlay and repays leisure care with daily joy. There are, as with other forms of gardening, certain rudimentary principles concerning the choice of containers, types of composts and fertilizers, support systems and tools. These topics and other routine chores are fully covered in the *Window Gardening* section.

The choice of plants for window gardening extends far beyond the ubiquitous geraniums, lobelias and petunias. The descriptions in the *Window Plants* section cover most of the popular as well as some of the more unusual subjects for window gardening, and, of course, there is never any harm in experimenting with others. The possibilities open to plant enthusiasts – even those with only a window sill – are endless.

Golden goblets

Of all the blooms which emerge to greet the first burst of spring sun, few can rival the crocus for sheer breathtaking beauty. Asking little from the gardener apart from reasonable soil, it appears year after year in ever-widening clumps to delight and astonish. The warm colour of a clay box shows off the goblet-like blooms to perfection, while an afterthought of white and lilac-striped crocuses serves to emphasize the edging of pure gold. When the foliage has died down, such large colonies ought to be lifted, separated and planted out in the garden, perhaps naturalized in grass; they can also be dried off and replanted, with wider spacings, in the window box in late summer.

The beauty of spring

Following the early show of snowdrops and crocus come hyacinths, sweetly scented and in pure colours of white and blue, yellow and pinkish-red. The massive types so popular for indoor flowering are best avoided in bedding schemes where they are exposed to strong winds and heavy rains. The wooden window box below is fitted with a zinc lining; when the hyacinths are over, the tray is simply lifted out and the bulbs removed to a place where they can die down undisturbed, and the box is ready for its summer occupants.

The golden trumpets of daffodils capture the very spirit of spring, lifting their bright faces to the sun without which they will not flourish. Year after year they fulfil the promise of spring, provided that they are allowed to complete their growing cycle and build up fresh resources. When the trumpets finally shrivel, lift the bulbs and transfer them to an out-of-the-way place where they can be left to die down naturally. Do not be tempted to remove the leaves from the bulbs before they have withered and turned completely brown.

Polyanthus primroses

One of the obscure ancestors of the large-flowered polyanthus was probably the small, yellow field primrose, whose botanical name is *Primula veris*, meaning first among spring flowers. Modern polyanthus strains have a complex parentage, but they are still harbingers of spring, and traces of the original species remain in the bright green, wrinkled leaves, the typical primrose flower shape and in the preference for moist soil and light shade. The large clusters of flowers now come in white, pale and deep yellow, pink, red, mahogany-brown and vivid blue. Compact of habit they are as much part of the early spring scene as snowdrops and crocus.

Cottage gardens

A tiny cottage, its thick stone walls weathered and mellowed through several centuries, captures a bygone age with a window adornment of pansies. The velvet-textured, open-faced violas, aptly called heart's-ease, are today as beloved as in Elizabethan times, though the colour range has expanded from the original purple, blue and yellow to include shades of red, mahogany and near-black. Closely related to the fragrant sweet violet, the scent of the modern pansy is more elusive, but as if in compensation it bears larger blooms and braves all kinds of weather.

Instant colour

A window dressing of evergreen
foliage plants gives year-round joy,
yet it occasionally cries out for odd
splashes of colour. At the window
opposite, pots of florist's broom and
dwarf pompon chrysanthemums
complement and strengthen glossy
viburnum foliage and variegated
sprawling euonymus. As the
pompons fade, they are replaced
with pots of heathers and spring
bulbs for winter and spring colour.
A narrow, shady window ledge
(*below*) is crammed with pots of
hydrangeas and chrysanthemums,
old favourites and in perfect
harmony with the old-fashioned
sash window and Victorian lace
curtain. Hemmed in by an ornate
railing, the pots, of clay rather than
lightweight plastic, are in no danger
of being blown over and will repay a
daily boost of water with months of
glowing colour.

Cool greenery

Softly filtered light creeps through windows shuttered against the glare of the noon sun. Evergreen ivies planted in deep troughs on the first balcony clothe the ochre walls, hide unsightly drain pipes and drape themselves from the railings of the upper balcony. Here the display continues with young, rapidly growing Boston ivy; freshly green and cool in summer, the wall becomes flames of brilliant scarlet, orange and deep golden in autumn before this deciduous climber sheds its glossy, three-lobed foliage, leaving behind a delicate tracery of self-clinging wiry stems.

Golden draperies

Most often seen as free-standing shrubs or multi-stemmed trees, laburnums make unusual and attractive wall plants, festooned in late spring and early summer with drooping chains of golden flowers, in effect not dissimilar to the blue-flowered wisteria. Training, which must begin with young plants, involves the removal of most horizontal branches until the required height of a single stem is reached. Thereafter a canopy is allowed to develop along supporting wires fixed to the house wall. Once the framework is established and the overhead branches interlaced, unwanted and wayward shoots should be trimmed back annually after flowering.

A company of clematis

Mention clematis, and the mind pictures flamboyant climbers with huge open-faced blooms which have all but obliterated the distinctive true species. One of the latter is *C. texensis* (*left*), native to Texas and magnificent with its pitcher-shaped, scarlet-red flowers which nod from the twining stems throughout the summer and autumn. It needs a warm and sheltered wall and even then is often of herbaceous habit, dying back to the ground in winter but appearing again in spring where a thick winter mulch has protected the root area.

'Hagley Hybrid' (*below*) belongs to the sturdy, fast-growing jackmanii group. From early summer onwards, it smothers its stems with a profusion of satin-pink flowers, conspicuous for their purple-brown anthers. Like others in this group, it mixes happily with climbing roses; the two can be pruned simultaneously in spring and urged to renewed splendour with a generous organic feed. The delicate pink colour, most effective against a white wall, tends to fade in strong sun, and a west-facing site is the most suitable.

Basement bargains

Many city basements are dark and dingy and there is little that will cheer them, but where even a small amount of light penetrates down to them there is little to deter the keen gardener. White-painted walls help to reflect the sun, and in such diffused light will flourish a veritable jungle of plants: pelargoniums, flame nettles, silver-leaved cineraria, French marigolds, wax and tuberous begonias, fuchsias, gloxinias, hydrangeas, petunias, lobelias and busy Lizzies or patient Lucy. Adding height to the riotous medley, a leafy passion flower winds its way upwards.

Summer in Tyrol

Small window boxes, safely anchored to the sills, brim with a sea of pink and scarlet pelargoniums, startling in their intensity against the white house walls. They are almost a superfluous embellishment to the lovingly carved window frames and doorway were it not for the reverent tribute they pay to the wall painting. A common feature in many small alpine villages, religious motives are especially found in Oberammergau, home of the famous Passion Plays performed by the villagers every ten years since the middle of the 17th century, as a thanksgiving for deliverance from the plague.

Hanging baskets

Brimming with gay summer flowers, hanging baskets bring a new dimension to window gardens; they break up a flat surface and set it alive. All baskets should be sheltered from strong winds and ideally have pulley systems to facilitate essential daily watering. The basket below is planted with trailing petunias, pelargoniums, nemesias, alyssums and lobelias; at the top cerise pelargoniums round off the arrangement.

Trailing plants, foliage and flowering, are indispensable for hiding the sides of baskets, arching plants for giving them height. Pelargoniums, fuchsias in their many varieties, nasturtiums, ferns and ivies are obvious choices and more commonly seen than the yellow-flowered creeping Jenny and the variegated wandering jew. The hanging garden below is a joy for the beholder, though something of a chore for the gardener: on sunny days the baskets need water more than once a day; during rainy spells they may flood.

Riotous colours

Basking in full sun, window boxes, deep and safely anchored, brim with colour throughout summer. Sweetly scented alyssum and trailing lobelia tumble over the edges, a froth of white and purple-blue against cerise and lavender petunias, golden-yellow calceolarias and red and white miniature roses. Sheltered by them from sudden gusts of wind, annual carnations, gladioli and lilies give height to the composition, while at ground level a tub of fuchsia and silver-leaved cinerarias provides depth and softens the straight outline of the boxes. On the left, a pot of ice plants will add soft, rosy colour in late summer.

Painted in pastel

Light and airy like a summer breeze,
a symphony of delicate colours has
been created round a clump of pale
salmon-pink petunias backed by
tingling fuchsia bells only one shade
deeper. Planted in the wings are
graceful marguerites and in the front
line sweet alyssums nudge lavender-
pink ageratums and trailing lobelias.
None are frost-hardy, but planted in
early summer they will flower for
months given a daily soaking, an
occasional feed and careful snipping
out of faded flowers. With care the
perennial fuchsia and marguerites
can be overwintered indoors and
coaxed into fresh bloom the
following summer.

Plants in pots

Lining an Italian balcony and affixed to the railings are clay pots of pelargoniums at various stages of growth, from rooted cuttings to mature plants in full bloom. Clay pots are less likely than plastic ones to topple over in sudden gusts of wind, but they also dry out faster. In more temperate climates, the potted oleander would have to be taken indoors to overwinter.

More potted pelargoniums (*right*) cheer up a dilapidated house front. The plastic pots are tightly wedged into drip trays that protect passers-by from getting soaked. The pelargoniums and carnations are fairly tolerant of drought and more likely to suffer from wet than from dry roots.

Unmistakably Mediterranean, an open window space is filled with a haphazard collection of potted plants (*far right*) – a love of plants taking priority over available light indoors. The terracotta pots mix comfortably with those in glazed ceramics and sport fuchsias and leggy carnations.

Window herbs

A sunny window sill outside the kitchen window is tailor-made for a handy collection of culinary herbs. From left to right are pots of lemon-scented thyme, spicy summer savory, velvety but astringent sage, and feathery, anise-like dill. A pot of sweet basil, indispensable in Mediterranean cooking, stands between two clumps of mint whose tendency to take over a conventional herb garden is curtailed within the confines of the pots. All are hardy, easily-grown perennials and annuals, except basil, which will not tolerate frost. Other good pot herbs include parsley and chervil, out of direct sun, chives, coriander and marjoram, and for culinary and ornamental purposes, bay and rosemary.

Pure sophistication

Simply designed white urns, raised on tall, slender plinths, appear made to order for a magnificent display of pelargoniums. With admirable restraint the colour scheme is limited to soft cerise in the upright flower fountain and pales to lavender-pink in low-growing types between the two urns. Daily watering and dead heading are musts to keep the arrangements in peak condition. At the end of the summer, small-leaved variegated ivies and deep pink or soft purple winter-flowering heaths can replace the summer blooms for long-lasting winter colour.

Youth and age

Morning glory scrambles its weak stems upwards at an astonishing speed (*left*) as if eager to reach the house roof before its single growing cycle comes to a close. And it still has surplus energy to produce a wealth of flower trumpets – scarlet, purple or blue – stark in relief against pale house walls, unfolding them in the morning and closing them at noon. For many summer months, it twines its graceful garlands round windows and doorways, exuberant as only youth can be, unaware that all glory is transient.

Wisteria (*right*) is quite the opposite. It belongs to large, mellow house walls but takes its time, feeling no urge to bloom prematurely and spending the formative years in establishing the strong roots and sturdy woody branches which will endure for a hundred years and more. When the time is ripe, wisteria, whose bare branches look almost dead in winter, festoons itself with sweet-scented lavender, blue or white flower drapes of such glorious and majestic splendour that early each summer belies its age.

40

Brilliant exotics

Brazil is the homeland of the
spectacular bougainvillea, and only
in near-tropical or Mediterranean-
type climates will it reach similar
proportions in the open. There it
twines its thorny stems over
archways, porches and house walls,
cascading its flower clusters in an
explosion of brilliant colour. The
'blooms' are in fact modified leaves,
in texture like silky paper tissue,
which completely obscure the true,
tiny and whitish flowers. In less
favoured regions, bougainvilleas
can be trained up greenhouse or
conservatory walls, to drape
themselves in summer over sunny
windows. Stained glass creates an
artistic centrepoint and during the
dormant season recalls the
splendour to come.

Rustic charm

The contrast between dark-stained wood cladding and pure white window frames is minimized and softened with a deep box brimming with purple lobelias. The rather sombre effect is offset with a huge cluster of white petunias and studded with scarlet pelargoniums. A hanging basket of lobelias alleviates the otherwise horizontal line and a three-dimensional picture is completed with a tub of fuchsias at ground level. The colour scheme of scarlet and pale pinkish-mauve complements that of the window box, creating a pleasing unity of apparent simplicity which will last the summer through.

Co-ordinated designs

A leaf-green wall paints the perfect backdrop for a thoughtful scheme of scarlet pelargoniums, white petunias and pinkish-blue lobelias. Two standard bay laurels, in strategically placed tubs, frame the picture; in time the climbing rose, planted in a deep wall basket, will drape its flower garlands over door and window.

Red and white are also the chosen colours in this stylish window arrangement (*below*), but the effective use of permanent foliage plants assigns to the short-lived bedding plants a secondary role. Rich contrasts in leaf shape, colours and habit are evident in trailing stems and feathery plumes, with the hanging basket foreshortening the long and narrow window.

An ornamental stone urn (*below*) becomes the focal point in a harmonious pink and white planting and draws the eye upwards to the window box, where the colour theme is repeated. An easy-to-assemble mix of pelargoniums, trailing lobelias and petunias, plus a centrally placed fuchsia to add height to the window box, make up the planting scheme.

Town elegance

Against a background of white and black, a window box bedded with bright red zonal pelargoniums, dainty white marguerites, and trailing, small-leaved variegated ivies adds a touch of timeless elegance. The colour theme is repeated in two deeper boxes flanking the front door and expanded in the permanent and evergreen occupants of dwarf pines, Lawson's cypresses and arching pyracanthas. In autumn and winter the red and white colours are maintained with clusters of colourful berries on the pyracanthas and in the silvery foliage of graceful silver-leaved cineraria nestling above more trailing ivies.

Silver for contrast

Foliage shrubs are invaluable as a foil for flowering plants, be it for the shape, texture or colour of their leaves. Silver-leaved cineraria combines all three features, with leaves as intricately cut as a filigree pattern, velvety to the touch and cool silvery-white in colour. In this handsome box it highlights the ornamental flower garlands, softens the begonias' brilliantly scarlet blooms and the fuchsias' purple-red bells. The glossy green begonia foliage appears almost polished close to the matt–white silver. In window boxes, all three subjects are best treated as bedding plants, although the silver-leaved cineraria will survive most winters outdoors.

Balcony bounty

Common to these balconies is lack of space for lounging and sitting, but there the similarity ends. Each displays a different mood even though the pelargonium is once again the central theme. The delicate tracery of the window grille on a Madrid town house (*below*) retains its prominence, the subdued flower display hiding only the footings.

A block of flats in central Copenhagen (*right*) identifies with that fun-loving city. Plants spill with cheery abundance from every space, oblivious of the daily arguments between flat-dwellers over untimely 'showers' from above. Such difficulties could be avoided with tailor-made boxes fitted with waterproof liners.

The bright red pelargoniums massed along the window railings (*right*) face no such problems, for the house overlooks the Atlantic. The sunny island of Madeira boasts an equitable climate where pelargoniums are just a few among a host of exotic plants. Their colours bright against sun-bleached walls, they promise a welcome as warm and as friendly as the islanders'.

A profusion of petunias

Pelargoniums and petunias vie for
the popularity stakes in container
gardening, with petunias claiming
the greatest variety in colour
combinations and only reluctantly
admitting to a few drawbacks.
Adorning this balcony garden with
a riot of blue and violet, lavender,
pink, red and white trumpets, some
frilly edged and others double-
petalled, they belie their animosity
to strong winds and heavy rain
squalls. The extra large Grandiflora
petunias are less suitable for exposed
positions than the trailing Pendula
types. From a distance no trace can
be seen of the sticky honeydew left
by the aphids to which they play
generous hosts unless the gardener
takes timely precautions.

The ubiquitous geranium

Commonly and mistakenly known
as geraniums, the ever-popular
scarlet, pink, white, lavender,
purple and bicoloured bedding
plants which fill the majority of
window boxes and baskets, pots
and containers are correctly named
pelargoniums. By any other name –
regal, zonal or ivy-leaved – they are
favourites from Spain to Sweden,
from Mexico to Montana, as they
trail or stretch their stems with an
unceasing succession of bloom. In
temperate climates they succumb to
frost, but happily switch from an
outdoor to an indoor sunny
window sill.

Lasting impressions

The stately cordylines (*left*) were introduced to Britain during the reign of Queen Victoria. Though hardly the original plants, they seem to embody the austere dignity of that era, framed like guards of honour beneath a gleaming canopy supported by ornate wrought-iron pillars. The evergreen foliage is barely ruffled by seaside winds nor affected by salt-laden sprays.

Some evergreens, such as variegated aucuba, the dark green false castor oil plant, and trailing ivy (*right*) are almost indestructible. They will survive in the most inhospitable situations, in deep shade and poor dry soil, tolerate the dust and grime of city life and shrug off lashing rainstorms.

In contrast to cordylines, the hardy bamboos (*below*) are vigorous and rampant growers, though the confines of a deep window box will check this tendency for a while. Of airy grace, the lush green grassy leaves tremble in the breeze, but bend and break in strong winds.

Evergreen walls

The common ivy will grow anywhere, trail its stems or climb a support, flourish in shade or sun, withstand drought and winter frost and react to hard pruning by putting out new stems clothed with fresh green, heart-shaped leaves. All it needs is a little initial encouragement: decent, well-drained soil at the foot of a wall, cane or plastic-wire supports to get it started on its way up, and an occasional boost of fertilizer during the growing season. Once established it attaches itself tenaciously to the wall with small aerial roots. Left to its own devices ivy will eventually replace its juvenile foliage with coarser, darker green leaves on stiff woody stems which can damage guttering and eaves with their sheer weight. For this reason, wall-trained ivy should be pruned in spring, cutting vigorous shoots back hard to the desired direction and shape, thus inducing new shoots with juvenile leaves to sprout.

Bold and beautiful

Regal or zonal, ivy or oak-leaved,
the progenitors of the numerous
pelargonium hybrids hail from
South Africa. Nowhere do they
flourish as exuberantly as when
basking in full, bright sun, raising or
trailing their stems and responding
to the warmth and glare with a
ceaseless burst of bloom. Few
compositions can be more effective
– or more easily created – than rows
of bright red zonal pelargoniums
standing guard over their ivy-leaved
cousins trailing their stems decked
with cerise-pink and white flower
clusters. Protected by both,
petunias, from another tropical
continent, flare their violet-purple
trumpets.

Sweet days of roses

As daffodils herald the spring so roses proclaim summer, responding to the warmth of the sun with months of bloom. Pygmy or giant, sprawling on the ground or reaching to the sky, bud after bud springs into full summer bloom, dazzling of form, heady of scent. Pink and white climbing roses (*below*) transform a small town balcony into a veritable bower of exquisite beauty and fragrance.

In complete contrast, but living proof that small is beautiful, miniature roses (*below*) are perfect in window boxes. At such close quarters the beauty of their blooms can be truly appreciated, and their daily maintenance becomes a labour of love.

A wall of pink roses (*right*), three storeys high, affirms the tenacity and longevity of the old-fashioned climbers. The carefully trained framework of main branches supports young side-shoots which, after spring pruning, each year festoon themselves with blossom.

The incomparable rose

Bare and gaunt in winter, clothed with vicious thorns on whipping stems which demand strong ties, recurrent attacks by blackflies and mildew – all is forgiven for the bewitching display of bloom in summer. There are climbing roses for walls of any aspect, including north, and blooms ranging from the simple, five-petalled types to blousy cabbage roses; some are borne shyly but daintily among the glossy foliage, others in exuberant clusters. They come in every conceivable shade of white and cream, yellow, golden and apricot, blush-pink, blood-red and scarlet, and many of the old-fashioned roses, like the one opposite, combine strong scent with perfection of bloom, while others follow the floral show with handsomely coloured hips.

Potted up

A tiny country cottage, immaculate
with white-washed walls and black
painted timbers, has adorned its
windows and doors with a veritable
forest of greenery. From pots of all
shapes and sizes tumble well-loved
cottage favourites like trailing
fuchsias, regal and zonal
pelargoniums, tuberous begonias
and variegated periwinkles. For
foliage contrast there are the arching
fronds of bright green buckler ferns
(*Dryopteris*), elegant strap-shaped
New Zealand flax, the sprawling
silvery stems of *Senecio* × 'Sunshine'
and, rising majestically close to the
door, a camellia of tree-like
proportions. Before the onset of
winter they will all be moved to
warmer quarters, to emerge freshly
repotted the following spring, to
bedazzle once again the passers-by.

Container planting

Boxes, troughs and containers at different levels give depth to a large and flat expanse of glass (*below*). Sharp outlines are blurred, angles distorted, and the overall effect is one of quiet dignity. A group of trumpet lilies holds the centre stage in a predominant colour scheme of soft blue, yellow and white, with silvery foliage plants muting the various shades of green. Although most are annual and bedding plants, they will maintain their display uninterrupted from early summer until the first autumn frosts.

Lack of ground space (*right*) is no impediment to the dedicated window gardener. From a trellis attached to the wall hang pots, baskets and half-pots packed with pelargoniums, trailing lobelias and begonias. The white plastic containers are unobtrusive and less prone to dry out than clay pots and open-wire baskets. Two conifers, sentinels by the door, add a touch of sobriety to the flamboyant colours, serene in the knowledge of their continued role when all the blooms have faded.

Carefree in the sun

Week after week, from early
summer into autumn, the small
Livingstone daisies from the African
veldt open their faces to the touch of
bright sun. The delicacy of their
blooms, ranging from pastel shades
to vivid colour combinations,
betrays nothing of the obstinacy
with which they overcome salty sea
breezes and near neglect; only in
dull, overcast weather do they hide
their dainty heads between the
sugar-frosted, succulent leaves.
Unlike the moisture-loving
hydrangea – still green in bud before
opening bright pink –
mesembryanthemums thrive in dry
soil, massed in shallow boxes and
other containers.

Down Mexico way

Small windows, set deep to keep the rooms behind them cool in the Mexican midday heat, are dressed with bright green zonal pelargoniums and baskets of trailing ivy. In such sun-drenched spots pelargoniums will respond by flowering almost unceasingly. The array of pots picks up and reflects the earthy-brown colour of courtyard and archway in whose shade flourish a magnificent Boston sword fern, and busy Lizzie or patient Lucy richly studded with cerise-pink blooms. Only in warm regions will these two assume similar proportions; in temperate climates the fern in particular will not tolerate winter outside.

Shades of purple

Mauve and violet-purple colours can be difficult to integrate in a limited space. The sombre solidity they create must be broken up and relieved with softer tones and outlines. The dot plants of silver-leaved cineraria used here (*left*) enhance and soften the purple scheme of lobelias and petunias.

The flower spikes of *Anchusa azurea* (*below*) are so loosely branched and airy that the intense blue of each individual flower is diffused among the light green foliage. These deep-rooted perennials are unusual but useful plants for a sunny position.

This window box (*below*) solves the problem of little space and deep shade with a compatible planting of campanulas and pink saponaria.

Window wizardry

A minimum of space need not deter the plant lover from expressing imagination and artistic flair. A deep terracotta pot holds a young wisteria, carefully trained on white-painted trellis; in years to come its intensely mauve-blue flower clusters will drape themselves from above both windows. Shading the wisteria roots, without depriving them of nourishment, are scarlet zinnias, rosemary and trailing lobelias. On the window sills are pots of pink and yellow petunias with, on the left, scarlet tobacco plants, heady with fragrance throughout the day. More lobelias trail beneath carnations and a glossy camellia, not perhaps the happiest companions for long – carnations relishing limy soil and camellias abhorring it.

The gnomes of suburbia

Smiling enigmatically and oblivious of their dwarf stature, the garden gnomes are there to stay, long after the pelargoniums and lobelias, the marigolds and fuchsias have faded from memory. Unaffected by weather, impervious to attacks by pests and diseases, the chief enemies are occasional street vandals and aesthetic-minded traditionalists.

In the pink

The tiniest gesture can have
dramatic impact: a pink-washed
cottage (*left*), with white-painted
old-fashioned sash windows,
becomes a visual backdrop for the
carefully positioned pink
pelargonium. The effect is
increased with white curtains.

Deep bowls of peonies (*right*), filled
with silky petals of palest shell-pink,
glisten proudly against mellowed
red brick. The flowering season
coincides with that of wisteria. The
annual spell of magic and glory
may be brief, but their beauty is
incomparable. With each passing
year the natural harmony of house
and plants becomes more evident.

Pink and white have also inspired
this romantic composition (*below*).
Candy-striped curtains are bunched
around a window seat from which
the gaze can roam across a window
box filled with pink and white
pelargoniums.

Snow-white and cool

Refreshingly cool on sultry summer days, white petunias raise their trumpets against a bright green background of pelargonium foliage. Intolerant of frost and somewhat frustrated by heavy rain and strong summer gales, they will bloom until the *Cotoneaster horizontalis*, planted against the foot of the wall, line their herring-bone branches with tiny, bright red berries. Undeterred by temperamental weather conditions, creeping Jenny tumbles its flower-coated evergreen stems like a bright yellow waterfall over the edges of the box. Pelargoniums and more petunias punctuate the cool scheme with vivid scarlet and deep violet-blue, with delicate marguerites on feathery stems nodding their approval from above.

Silvery succulents

Where summers are warmer and light more intense than usually experienced in northern gardens, succulents make striking window-box subjects. The silvery types in particular (*right*) appear cool and restful and include such easy growers as *Kleinia haworthii*, the burro's tail, with trailing stems of teardrop leaves and, also trailing, toothed and four-sided stapelia.

The ghost plant (*Graptopetalum paraguayense* or *Sedum weinbergii*) is almost bluish-white (*below*) against flowering mesembryanthemums and ivy-leaved pelargoniums. At the top a miniature tree, a purple-leaved aeonium lifts its succulent leaf rosettes which have matured from silver-white to near coppery-purple. Come autumn, and the succulents are taken indoors.

Balconies in miniature

Tiny windows lacking even a ledge can still be decorated with a few pot plants. A lightweight metal tray secured to the window frame can accommodate gay pelargoniums or those house plants that relish a summer spell in the open air. Several succulents, among them the Christmas and Easter cacti respond especially well to outdoor summer quarters, where bright sun can harden the young, flat leaf joints. They must, however, be brought indoors before the onset of autumn because flower buds are only initiated when hours of darkness exceed those of daylight.

Summer's end

As if ignorant of shortening days
and waning sun, the flame nettles or
coleus in this window box live up to
their name by continuing their
colourful display of pink, red,
bronze and gold. To prevent the
plants from 'bolting' the
insignificant bluish-white flower
spikes should be pinched out as soon
as they appear. Although flame
nettles will succumb to the first
frost, they can be perpetuated
through tip cuttings which root
easily in water and which can be
overwintered indoors to await the
coming of another spring. Then,
too, the silky seed heads on the
clematis will have dispersed on the
wind, to give way to a fresh crop of
bloom simultaneously with the
wall-trained wisteria.

Window vegetables

French and kidney beans are marvellous in pots and boxes outside sunny and sheltered windows. Runner beans (*left*) need deeper pots, such as balcony tubs with trellis or cane framework; trained up strings their red or white flower curtains are followed by succulent pods, ready for picking. Spray the plants with soft water when the flowers appear, to assist pollination.

Several cucumber varieties (*above*) are specially bred for window-sill pot culture and repay good light, frequent watering and feeding with a healthy crop of fruits; remember to remove all male flowers as they appear, to avoid the typical bitterness which results from cross-pollination.

Outdoor bush-type tomatoes thrive in tubs, pots and growbags on balconies or against sunny house walls. Lacking such opportunities, the small-fruited varieties (*left*) make handsome and tasty window-sill plants. The bite-sized fruits are sweet, juicy and thin-skinned and borne in abundance if the tomato plants are stopped when four flower trusses have set.

93

Autumn riots

True Virginia creeper clothes itself
in a dazzling mantle of fiery orange
turning to glowing scarlet before
falling softly to the autumn-wet
ground. Hardy and reliable, finding
a foothold in the tiniest crevice in
house walls and fences, this creeper
needs a restraining hand before it
obliterates doors and windows,
forces gutters from the roof and
chokes the chimney pots. Fading,
rusty-brown hydrangea mop heads
echo the vivid colours and persist
long after the creeper has shed its last
leaf and withdrawn to its winter
dormancy.

Gold and green cladding

The common ivy grows wild in many parts of Europe, scrambling up tree trunks, covering the forest floor and weaving along hedgerows. Almost as enduring as the ancient legends in which it features, common ivy has given rise to dozens of named varieties, all differing in leaf shapes and colours. 'Goldheart' is one of the most popular for wall coverings, being neat of habit, with small three or five-lobed leaves set closely along the stems and distinguished by a bright golden splash in the centre of each. Unlike all-green ivies, 'Goldheart', and other variegated types, are most conspicuous when grown in full sun.

Shaped to fit

Firethorn is fast-growing and with a little help will embellish any house wall in the space of a few years: the sturdy branches and small evergreen leaves tolerate hard pruning better than most. These two specimens here (*left*) are trained as standards, all side branches on the woody trunks below the upper-floor balcony being pruned out. The leaf canopy is trimmed lightly so as not to sacrifice the berry clusters.

Evergreen box (*below*) has long been a favourite subject for topiary enthusiasts. But novices should beware: topiary is an ongoing operation; once established, the shape must be maintained with meticulous use of secateurs twice in each growing season.

Pyracantha in autumn (*below*), with tier upon tier of orange-red berries. Such spectacular results occur only after careful pruning, done when the blooms have faded. All new shoots are cut back to just above a flower cluster.

Living architecture

The Romans were masters of the ancient art known as topiary, in which evergreen trees and shrubs are pruned to ornamental, often bizarre and mythical shapes. Many more recent examples of the art are still to be seen in great gardens today. Soft-leaved conifers like cypress and yews were the original favourite materials, but several other evergreens respond equally well to the artistic imagination of the skilled topiarist. Here pyracantha has been painstakingly shaped, with the aid of a wire frame, into a row of fanciful stars.

Winter cheer

Evergreens are essential for the
dreary days of winter. Skillfully
positioned they can assume
dramatic impact, the foliage stark
against a white background, the
seemingly artless composition a
visual entity of quiet dignity. Here,
fronds of cabbage palm rise like a
fountain above ripples of trailing
ivies, green and variegated, and
flanked on either side by soft green
sentinels of dwarf Lawson's
cypress. Sprawling stems of winter
cherry weave their gay garlands of
bright red berries among the
greenery. Hard frost may kill off the
cabbage palm and the winter cherry,
but before long early crocus,
nestling below them, will thrust up
their golden blooms.

Under cover

Snug inside a covered porch, flowering plants framed in arched windows bring more than a passing hint of the coming spring (*left*). Pots of crocus, cinerarias, primulas and cyclamen brighten the view from outside and inside the house, responding to the light and to the cool temperature with a long-lasting colour display. Such a position is ideal for cyclamen, which, though never frost-hardy, dislike the heat of a living-room.

The bird of paradise flower (*Strelitzia reginae*) (*below*) prefers conservatory treatment if it is to live up to its exotic name. In late spring, the leathery leaves become a foil for spectacular flowers which emerge like crested birds' heads of bright orange and vivid blue, though it rarely flowers before six years old.

Indoor window sills

Window dressing is not confined to outdoor embellishments. Snug behind glass and lit by late winter sunshine, indoor pot plants hint at the promise of warmer days and meanwhile fill their place of pride with magnificent blooms. Given the cool position of a window sill, away from blasts of central heating, indoor cyclamen will raise their shuttlecock blooms high above marbled leaf rosettes. The delicacy of their flowers only serves to emphasize the robust hyacinth spikes, pure white and sweetly fragrant. Specially treated for early indoor blooming, hyacinth bulbs can be transplanted to the garden or outdoor window boxes for flowering the following spring.

Bright outlooks

A tall and narrow window might seem difficult to decorate, but when it faces south (*left*) it becomes the perfect site for those plants that revel in bright sun. Desert cacti and succulents mix with variegated house plants whose colours develop best in sun. Trailing foliage relieves what might be a static arrangement, and glass shelves ensure that all plants receive maximum light.

Similar treatment has been given to the window below and resulted in a garden which looks equally attractive viewed from inside and out. The wooden shelves have metal liners to prevent water damage, and in the good but diffused light thrive such plants as philodendrons, marantas, purple velvety gynuras, trailing scindapsus and spathiphyllum with its glossy green leaves and tall elegant flowers.

Indoor greenery

Window dressing is not confined to the outside. Small apertures which serve no purpose other than letting in light to dark stairwells (*above*) can become focal points of interest by careful juxtaposition of indoor plants: the false castor oil plant is truly happy in such a situation. The suffused light throws its luxuriant foliage into bright silhouette.

These plants lend a tropical air to a well-lit window sill (*right*). The avocado pear on the left, rewarding patience with a canopy of lush greenery, casts dappled shade over the pretty little maidenhair fern, whose filigree foliage objects to strong light. Meanwhile the variegated abutilon responds to the sun with a wealth of lantern-shaped flowers drooping from the stems.

WINDOW GARDENING

The imaginative and successful plantings shown on pages 7-111, casual as they may seem, derive their stunning and lasting effects from attention to several practical details: the choice of container, the correct compost, the right amount of watering, deadheading, pruning, and the prevention of pests and diseases. This is not as daunting as it may sound – thought and care, rather than skill, are all that are required. If the simple advice given below is followed, even the least experienced gardener will succeed.

Choosing containers

First, where are you going to grow your plants? If directly into the ground, all well and good – though the soil close to house walls is usually extremely dry. This is due to water absorption by the foundation, as well as to shelter provided by the wall itself and overhanging eaves and gutters. So plant well clear of the wall – some 12-15in(30-38cm) away – and then train stems of climbers and wall shrubs back to their support.

However, in many situations there is no suitable planting area. Maybe the ground is paved or the soil quite hopeless; or perhaps your 'garden' is a balcony. In such situations you must use containers of one sort or another – a blanket term covering pots, tubs, troughs, urns and window boxes.

Once the basic choice rested between earthenware, cast stone and timber. But plastics, including fibreglass, have now broadened the field dramatically. These materials are for the most part cheaper than traditional types, and containers made from them neither chip nor rot. There is much to be said for those with clean, smooth lines and no pretensions. Such containers do have the advantage of being easier to keep clean, for any splashed earth or general atmospheric dirt is less likely to stick to their sides, and washing is a simple matter. However, in spite of manufacturing ingenuity they seldom look other than what they are – plastic.

Stone containers (cast from reconstituted stone) are handsome, fairly expensive, and look splendid set alongside a period house but rather less so in a modern setting. Because of their weight, however, check with a local surveyor before burdening a balcony with them.

Unglazed pottery is always popular. Modern pots tend to have clean, functional lines, but always keep your eyes open at sales and house clearances for those splendidly ornate containers of yesterday. And don't overlook wall pots, many of even the modern ones having attractive patterns or a scalloped rim. An important aspect to consider is that earth and ceramic containers should be frostproof. Clay pots, particularly in regions subject to alternate freezing and thawing, are likely to crack unless properly fired and guaranteed to be frost-proof.

The overall limitation of earthenware, certainly for planting the most vigorous wall shrubs, is size. The biggest pots have a 20in(51cm) diameter, whereas a 30in(76cm) tub is about right for many shrubs and small trees. And they do dry out very rapidly.

In contrast, wooden containers – in the form of tubs, troughs or half-barrels – hold moisture quite well and therefore need less watering. Oak, iroko (African teak), redwood, cedar and types of mahogany are most widely used. These woods are very durable, especially if a metal or plastic liner is fitted to decrease the chances of rotting. Being a natural material, timber always looks 'right' with plants and such containers are made in sizes to suit plants with quite large root systems.

All really large containers should be capable of being moved for cleaning the surface on which they rest – if necessary using a system of levers and rollers. Or the container could be on castors.

Hanging pots and containers can be suspended from brackets attached to house walls. Hanging baskets and half-baskets can also be secured to a wall; the lining of black plastic sheeting needed to retain the compost can be concealed with sphagnum moss or straw placed between the plastic and the bars.

The choice of free-standing containers for your window garden is varied; they include half-barrels (1), stone urns (2) and pedestals (3), timber terrace boxes (4), plastic tubs and bowls (5, 7) earthenware strawberry-pots (6) and reconstituted stone troughs (8).

Choice of colour in containers arises mainly with plastic kinds, although there are some cast-concrete products with a multi-colour finish. In white, plastic is a safe choice, as are fawns and greens. Light-coloured pots and tubs have a positive advantage during the drearier times of year and they tend to be more acceptable close to the house than they might be in the garden proper.

Finally, there are window boxes, both for placing on sills and for supporting on wall brackets beneath the window. The choice here is more limited and you may not at once find something to your liking that will also match the window width or sill depth. Plain, white plastic is unobtrusive when placed on the sill of a white-painted window. Wooden boxes, the preferred choice in many cases, are less widely available and more expensive, so you might consider making your own.

For safety, secure each end of a window box with a long-arm hook attached to the frame or sill. For boxes supported on a sill, make wooden wedges and place them under the box to ensure that it does not tilt with the slope of the sill. The wedges will aid stability, but for complete safety the box should be prevented from falling by screwing metal angle pieces to the sill as shown in the illustration. Because of the slope of the sill the vertical arm of the angle piece will need to be bent towards the front of the box.

Support wall-mounted boxes on stout brackets – ornamental for preference, if they are above eye-level and exposed – screwed securely to the wall. The vertical arms of brackets may either be concealed behind the box (that is, pointing upwards), or point downwards beneath it. The shorter leg of each bracket should match the front-to-back measurement of the box, and there should be one bracket for about each 12in(30cm) of length, the outer ones being close to the ends. Secure the brackets to the wall with 1½in(4cm) screws (the precise type will depend on the kind of bracket), first drilling the wall with a suitable-sized masonry drill and inserting plastic wall plugs.

Making window boxes

A window box is really very easy to make, the advantage being that you can tailor it to fit a particular sill or width of opening. Use ⅞in(22mm) softwood for the sides, base and ends, aiming for a minimum overall height and depth (front and back) of 6in(15cm). Remember that the compost in a smaller box will dry out rather rapidly.

Cut the two end pieces with the grain vertical, and ⅞in(22mm) shallower and 1¾in(4.5cm) narrower than the overall size of the box end (to allow for them resting on the ends of the base and within the side panels). To reinforce the sides of a very long box, cut intermediate pieces of the same size as the ends

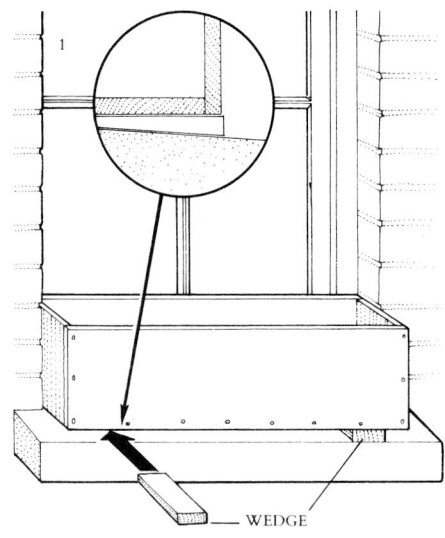

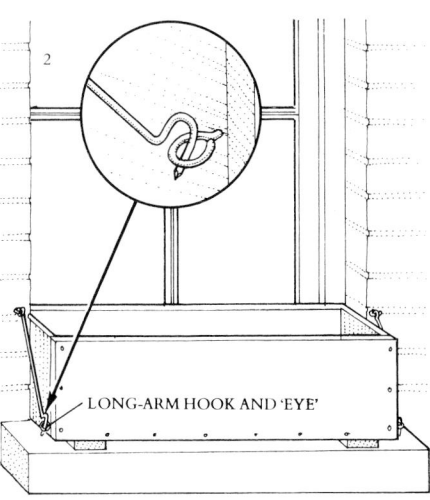

On a sloping sill insert compensating wedges under a window box (1). Use long-arm hooks and eyes to anchor the box to the frame or sill (2).

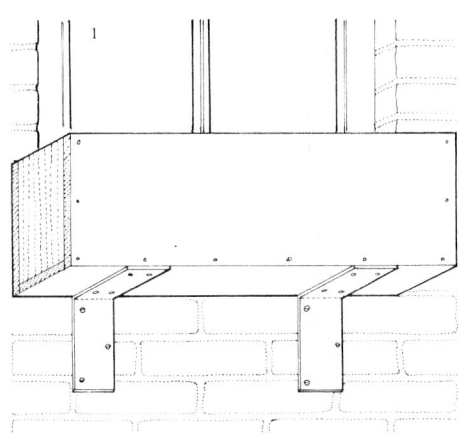

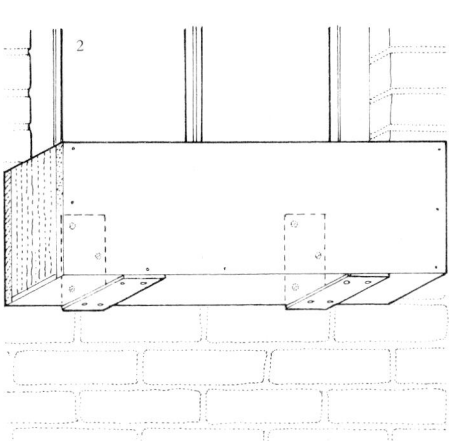

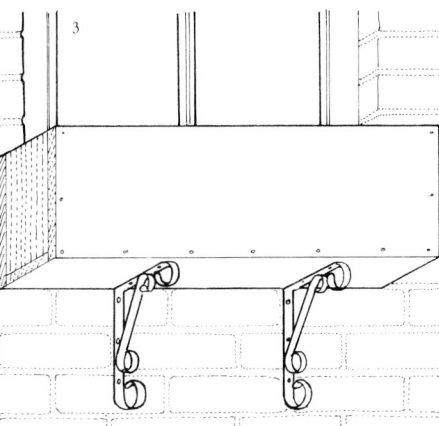

Wall-mounted window boxes may be secured by various means. If to be viewed at eye level or

lower, the brackets need not be particularly ornamental, and may be mounted below (1) or

concealed behind (2). Boxes viewed from below are best secured with ornamental brackets (3).

and place at 12-18in(30-46cm) intervals.

Drill and countersink pilot holes through the sides and base, in groups of three, to correspond with the positions of end and reinforcing pieces. Then, using brass screws, which do not rust, screw all the components together and fill the countersunk holes with a suitable wood filler. Bore ⅜in(1cm) drainage holes every few inches along the base.

Brush the inside and outside of the box liberally with a wood preservative that is not toxic to plants. Also, ensure that the sides of the drainage holes are well covered with the preservative to prevent moisture entering the wood. The box could also be painted with oil paint, using the time-honoured system of primer, undercoat and topcoat. You can prolong the life of the wood still further by lining the box with plastic or removable zinc trays before filling with compost. Perforate the lining above each drainage hole.

Soil mixtures and composts

The soil for the containers should preferably be sterilized and must contain sufficient nutrients for healthy growth. The best growing medium for all container plants is a loam- or peat-based potting compost – in the UK this means John Innes No. 2 for temporary plants, John Innes No. 3 for permanent subjects or the equivalent proprietary peat-based composts. In the USA similar mixtures are sold as general-purpose potting soil, the packaging indicating the proportions of essential fertilizers. A few lucky gardeners may have garden soil suitable for use, but, not being sterilized, it will contain weed seeds and may harbour pests and disease spores.

Bear in mind that some plants will not thrive in soil containing lime, which is included in all the proprietary composts. For this group of plants, including rhododendrons (azaleas), camellias and most heaths, you will need to purchase a lime-free, or ericaceous compost.

Plants in peat-based composts need supplementary feeding at an earlier stage than those in the loam composts.

Preparing and planting

Having chosen your containers, their preparation and planting is a fairly straightforward operation, the details of which are illustrated opposite. There are, however, a few general points worth making.

Do not, in an excess of enthusiasm, plant out tender varieties too early – late frosts or even cold winds will spoil your dreams of a perfect display.

Whether you have bought the plants as seedlings, pot-grown specimens or raised them yourself, it is a good idea to place them on the surface of the soil in the container or window box to work out your design before planting.

When planting large containers with a number of plants, start at the centre and work outwards. As a rule set the tallest plant or plants in the middle, with shorter or trailing varieties near the edges. But if planting a climber in a substantial container you may prefer to set this near the back (and the wall) and then arrange other plants around the front and sides. Set taller plants at the back of troughs and window boxes, shorter ones in front.

Make the most of climbing and trailing plants to increase the height of your display and to conceal the outline of containers. This is especially valuable with hanging baskets, wall-mounted containers and window boxes.

If your plants are to go directly into the ground, fork in a good dressing of moisture-holding humus, along with suitable plant foods. Leafmould or thoroughly rotted compost, for example, fortified with a handful or two of bonemeal is ideal. Otherwise, buy a bag of one of the proprietary planting mixtures, based on peat or shredded bark. Whichever type you use, mix in a generous amount all round the planting area rather than placing a handful in the bottom of the planting hole.

Choosing the plants

A wide range of plants is suitable for window gardening, with a large number described in the next section.

What you choose to grow is in many ways a personal matter, but there are a few factors that ought to be taken into account. How sunny or shady is your site? What will the plants you would

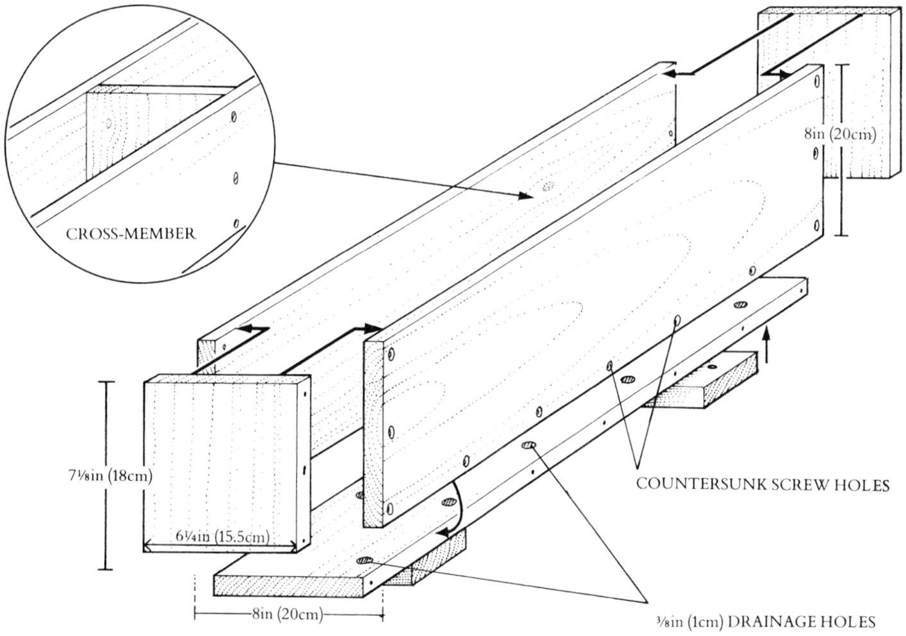

CROSS-MEMBER

7⅛in (18cm)

6¼in (15.5cm)

8in (20cm)

8in (20cm)

COUNTERSUNK SCREW HOLES

⅜in (1cm) DRAINAGE HOLES

Making a window box is really quite easy. This exploded diagram, together with the instructions above, show the essential components for constructing an 8in (20cm) deep timber box. Of course, the finished size of the box can be tailored to fit any size of window.

like to grow look like against the colour of the walls? Do you want the planting to be permanent, seasonal or a combination of the two?

Plants whose flowers open only in the sun would not be a good choice for a shady site; conversely, those that naturally like moist woodland conditions are unlikely to be happy in full sun. Also, some plants have transient flowers, at their best early in the day, so by the time you return home from work you would see only fallen petals.

Bulbs, hardy and half-hardy annuals, biennials, hardy and tender perennials, climbers, shrubs and small trees can all be used for window gardening and between them will provide all you need for colour and foliage effect.

Other than shrubs, planted for their permanent evergreen foliage or winter berries, the year may be said to begin with winter- and spring-flowering bulbs. Here there is a wide choice, including snowdrops, crocuses, miniature narcissi, bulbous irises and hyacinths. Although most prefer a sunny site, many will bloom in shade if fresh supplies are bought every year.

In the summer months the annuals are the mainstay. Many you can raise yourself from seed, while others, particularly if you have no garden, can be bought from nurseries, garden shops and chain stores. There are dozens of kinds, including trailing types.

Biennials such as forget-me-nots and wallflowers can be planted in early au-

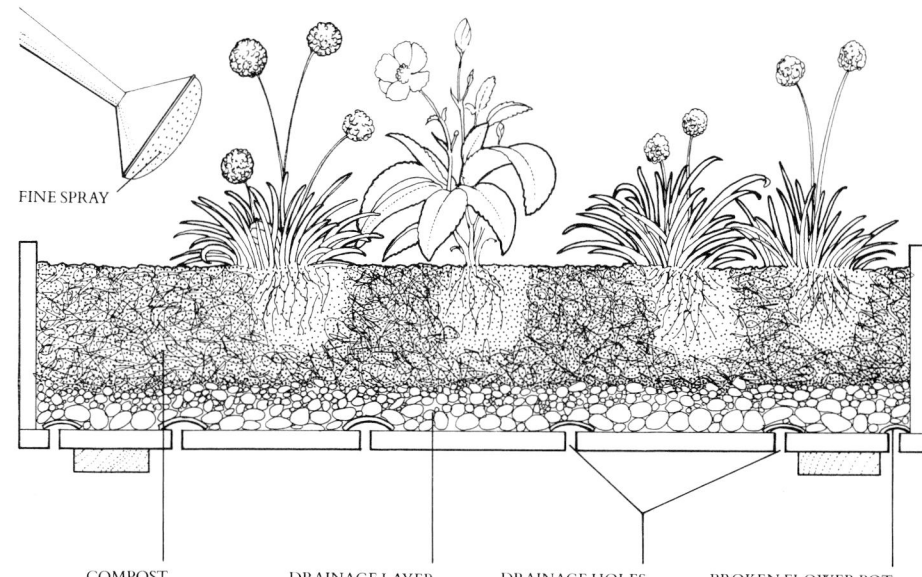

FINE SPRAY

COMPOST   DRAINAGE LAYER   DRAINAGE HOLES   BROKEN FLOWER POT

Always allow adequate drainage when planting a window box – bridge hole with broken flower pot

then add coarse sand or grit before filling in with compost. Water in new plants with a fine spray.

tumn after the summer bedding plants have served their purpose. To raise these from seed is not difficult, but you do need garden space, or you can buy them in as seedlings.

Hardy perennials – plants that are left undisturbed to make fresh growth each spring and then die down in the autumn – may not be an automatic choice for containers, certainly for small ones, but there are several useful varieties. More substantial perennials can be planted in the centre of a large tub, and some are so good that they make a feature in their own right. Taller varieties are useful for planting below windows.

No window garden would be complete without pelargoniums (geraniums), tender perennials that include varieties with brilliant hues, coloured and scented foliage, and trailing types. Grey-foliaged plants, some of which are tender, add much to any planting.

Small, compact shrubs and dwarf conifers form the backbone of a permanent planting. Choose ones with good foliage – either throughout the year, or in autumn. Many have berries as well as flowers. In the winter, variegated aucubas, winter cherries, heathers, blue-grey hebes and trailing ivies will make a substantial display.

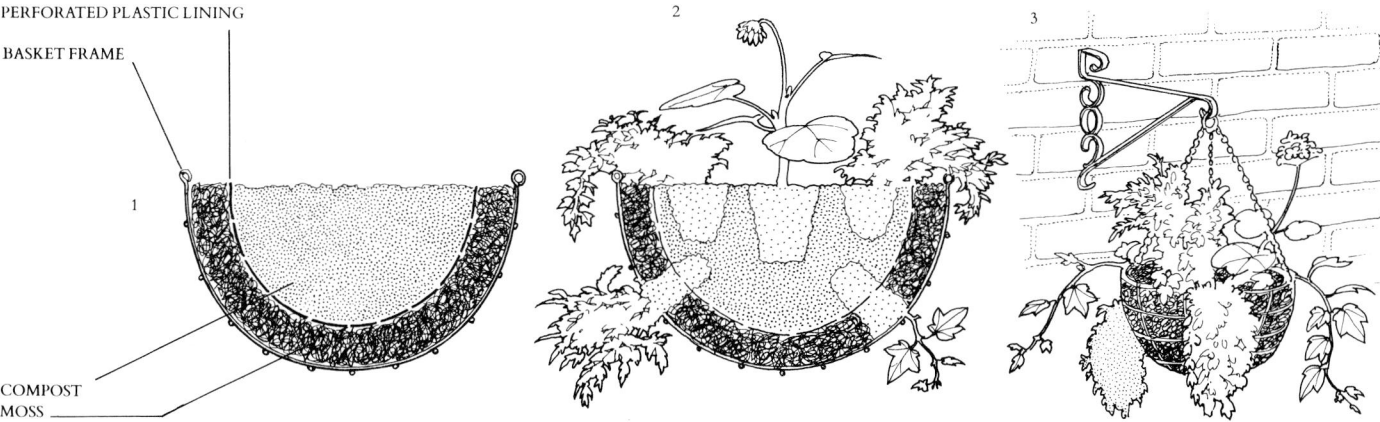

PERFORATED PLASTIC LINING

BASKET FRAME

1

COMPOST
MOSS

2

3

Moss looks most natural as a liner for hanging baskets – for best results add a layer of perforated

plastic (1). Position trailing plants at the edges or insert them through the sides (2). Plant upright

plants at the centre or back to add height. Water well before hanging up (3).

Climbers, whether woody or herbaceous, are essential around a window: roses for their scented flowers, clematis and everlasting peas for their colours and vines for their foliage and fruit are just a few.

If you sit out in your window garden or often pass through it you should consider using scented plants. Particularly valuable are sweet peas, flowering tobacco, wallflowers, verbenas, violets and hyacinths, and among the shrubs, honeysuckles, viburnums, many roses and lavender.

A window box is an excellent place for growing a selection of herbs. Or you could grow them as individual pot plants, spacing them to suit their different spreads. Among the more compact are chives, pot marjoram, mint (if the roots are restricted), parsley, sage and thyme. All need a sunny position and will thrive in well-drained compost. The possible exception is mint, which relishes moist soil.

Certain vegetables grow well in containers, for example tomatoes, lettuces, radishes and salad onions: it does not require a great deal of space to get worthwhile results. Climbers such as runner beans, and trailing marrows, grow rapidly, providing almost 'instant' greenery.

Strawberry pots and barrels, with holes in their sides for the plants, are both decorative and practical. They occupy comparatively little space, yield worthwhile crops and are easily covered with netting to protect the ripening fruit from birds.

Winter care

With the onset of autumn, most flowering plants are past their best. Annuals are discarded and replaced with spring-flowering subjects; herbaceous perennials, climbers and wall shrubs should be tidied, dead stems and leaves removed, stray shoots shortened and others tied in. Hardy plants will fend for themselves during the winter though some, such as trumpet vines, passion flowers and nerines, may need a precautionary straw or bracken mulch over the root area.

It is foolhardy to risk the survival of tender and prized container plants. Pots of agapanthus and some lilies appreciate frost-free winter quarters in a greenhouse, conservatory or a covered porch; these are also ideal situations for New Zealand flax and fuchsias. Keep the compost barely moist during the resting period and let it dry out between waterings. Tubs of camellias prefer similar treatment, but bud drop may occur if the roots dry out completely.

Truly tender plants will need more heat during winter: shrubby hibiscus, oleander and plumbago cannot be expected to survive unless given a minimum greenhouse/conservatory temperature of 45°F(7°C) and careful watering. Tender herbaceous plants, such as the tuberous begonias and cannas, must be lifted from their containers before the first autumn frost, dried off and cleaned of shrivelled foliage and roots. Store them in a frost-free place in boxes of peat; this should be just moist at all times – too dry and the tubers will shrivel, too wet and they will rot. In early spring, start them into growth with increased heat and watering.

Pelargoniums will not tolerate frost in early autumn, lift them from window boxes and containers, pot or box them in compost, cut them back and overwinter them at a temperature of 40°F(4°C) minimum. Very little water is required though dust-dry conditions should be avoided (some growers successfully overwinter the lifted plants rolled in newspaper and kept dark and dry). In spring, cut the plants back hard, increase watering and, as renewed growth appears, feed every fortnight.

House plants

Numerous popular books are available on the culture of indoor plants so they are not covered in detail here. However, as shown on pages 104-111, indoor plants are invaluable to the dedicated window gardener. The inside window space can be decorated with plants that harmonize with those outside, sweetheart plants can be trained round the frames, while sills can be filled with flowering and foliage plants.

Many house plants are suitable as outdoor container plants, and several relish a summer spent in the open, sunk in their pots in garden soil or in tubs or simply stood on sunny and sheltered balconies and patios. Spider plant and asparagus fern, *Campanula isophylla* and *Saxifraga stolonifera* are marvellous plants for hanging baskets.

Cacti and other succulents revel in sun and fresh air; poinsettias, azaleas and solanums ripen their shoots and form buds better outdoors.

Cordylines, pittosporums, myrtles, citrus plants and fatshederas give spectacular foliage emphasis to the outdoor window garden. They must all be moved back to indoor quarters at the end of the summer; for a week or two keep them separate from other plants in case they are harbouring pests.

Providing support

Climbers and other wall shrubs apart, many container-grown plants need some support. Raised above ground level, they are especially vulnerable to the wind, while close proximity to a building often results in fierce gusts and eddies. Young plants are particularly at risk, for movement hampers root establishment – especially in the case of shrubs and small trees.

It is essential to give support from the start. In firm ground, the easiest method is to insert a cane quite close to the main stem, securing it with soft twine. Make one or more figure-of-eight ties, which allow space for the stem to develop. Bushy plants may need two or three canes, with the twine criss-crossed between. Proprietary metal stakes, which may be used instead of canes, some with a linkage system for mutual support, are sometimes available though usually expensive.

In fairly shallow containers the compost may not provide a secure anchorage – especially for a single support. If doubling-up does not solve the problem, use one of the free-standing frames sold for supporting tomatoes and other plants when they are cultivated in growing bags. Or, with a little ingenuity, you can make your own by insert-

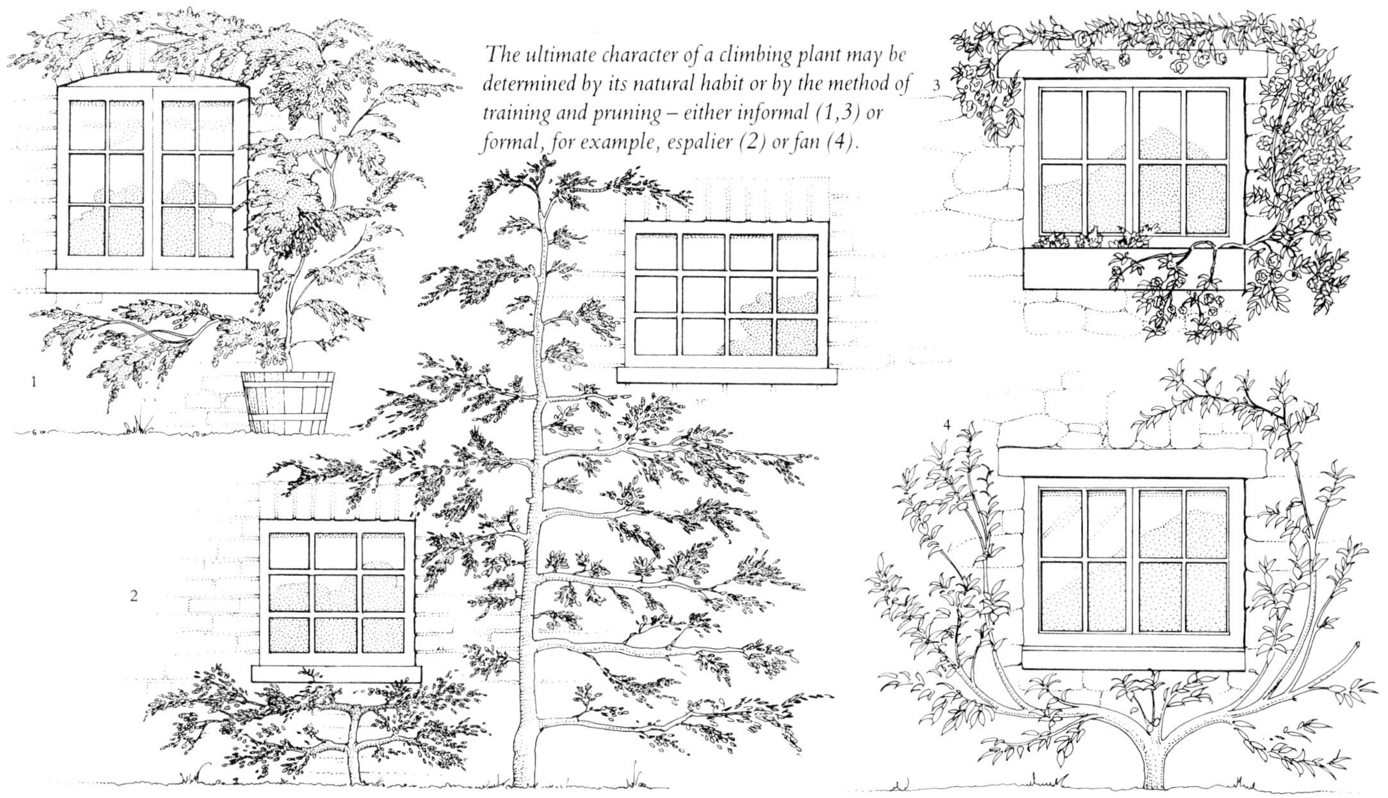

The ultimate character of a climbing plant may be determined by its natural habit or by the method of training and pruning – either informal (1,3) or formal, for example, espalier (2) or fan (4).

ing canes into holes drilled into heavy wooden blocks, with horizontal canes tied between.

Annuals and other small plants are less in need of support, but a few twiggy sticks pushed in between them will give more resistance to wind buffeting.

Best known of the self-clinging climbers are the ivies, and Virginia creepers. Both will grow against almost any wall, but they require support in their early years.

For wall plants, other than the self-clinging types, some form of fixed, permanent support is essential. This must be secured close to the wall, but allow space for air circulation and for stems to twist around, or be tied to, the support – insert pre-drilled blocks between frame and wall.

Wall plants that need additional support can be grouped into those that will support themselves by means of tendrils or by twining, and others – not really climbers at all – that have to be trained and tied in position.

Shrubs that become wall plants only when trained and supported are quite numerous. Popular kinds suitable for a

sunny wall include Californian lilacs, climbing roses and grape vines. Particularly good for a shaded wall are jasmine and pyracantha.

As for methods of support, trellis is one of the most useful and is manufactured in several shapes and patterns. In addition to square and diamond de-

signs, there are attractive fan-shaped types with a tall, narrow profile, useful where wall space is restricted and plants can be trained to an upright habit. As well as the traditional wooden trellis it is available in sections formed from thick wire with a plastic coating.

Plastic netting is a good alternative,

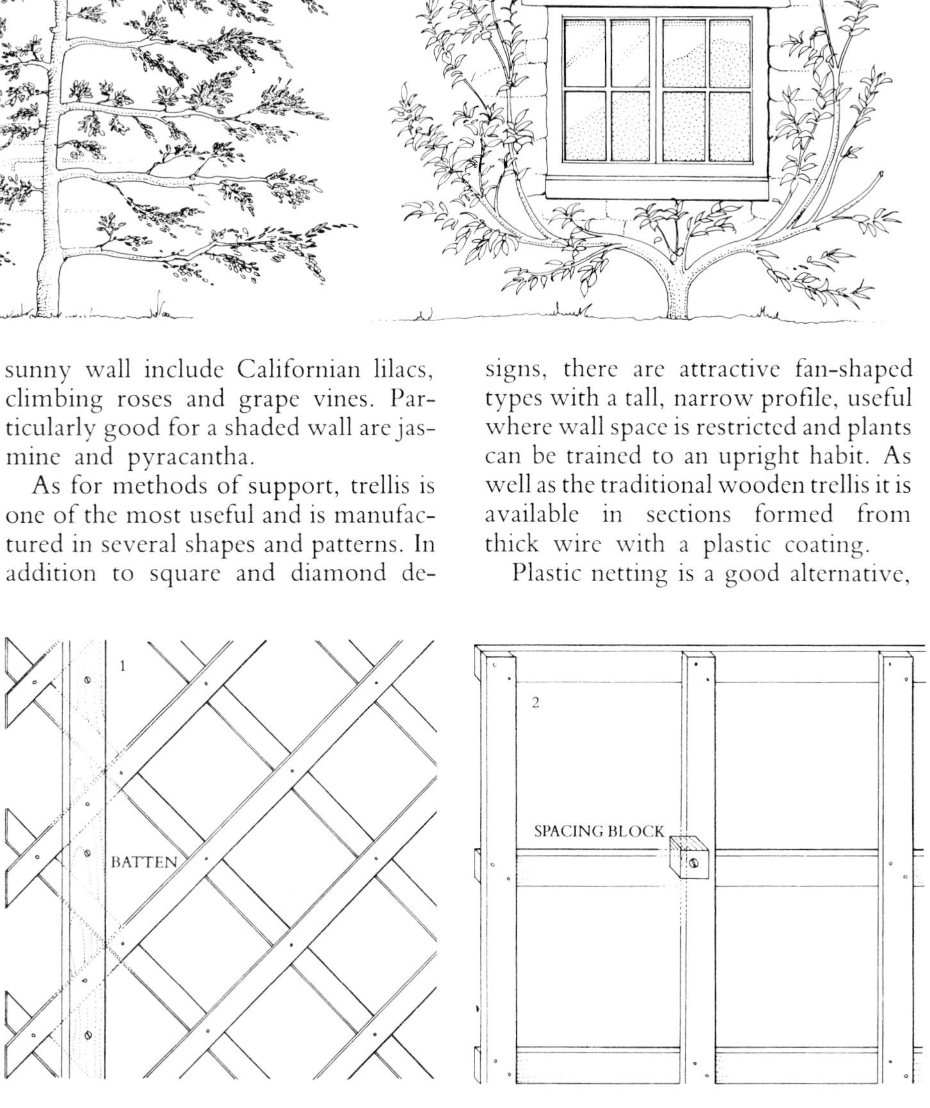

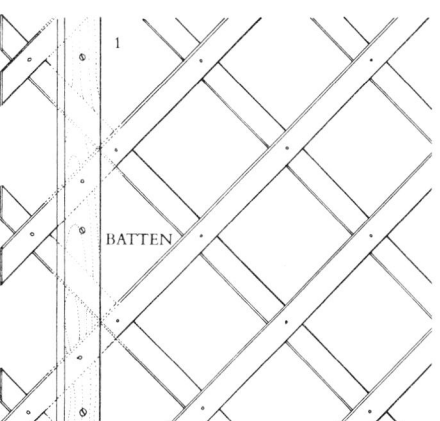

Trellis provides a useful means of rigid support for climbing plants. The design may be diamond (1) or square (2). Be sure to secure it slightly away

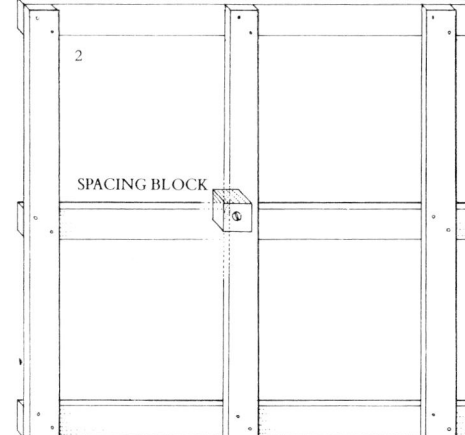

from the wall using either battens or spacing blocks, to allow plants room to intertwine through the trellis.

provided one of the large-mesh types is chosen. Sometimes called clematis support, this has a mesh about 2in(5cm) square or more and is easily fixed with patent plastic clips that support the netting well clear of the wall. Or, instead of plastic fixings, the netting can be stapled to wooden battens screwed to the wall. All-plastic mesh, available in green, white and tan, is cheaper than plastic-coated wire, is rot-proof and will last for years.

Less expensive than either trellis or mesh are wires fastened horizontally at about 1ft(30cm) intervals. These are also less conspicuous – especially compared with plastic mesh, which tends to be rather overpowering until covered by the plants. Wires may be secured directly to the wall with galvanized-iron vine-eyes or to vertical battens. Heavy-gauge wire must be pulled tight with a tensioning bolt at one end, but lighter wire can be tied directly on to the vine-eyes. Intermediate eyes or battens are needed at about 10ft(3m) intervals.

Not all climbing plants need to be grown against a wall, of course. Sweet peas are an obvious example, and it is easy to devise free-standing support with a cone or cylinder of wire netting, or else a wigwam of pea sticks. Decorative ivies can be trained up a simply made open-framed wooden obelisk or wigwam.

Watering and damping down

Container-grown plants depend on hand-watering for survival. Though little or none may be needed during a damp spell, the compost will start to dry out almost as soon as the rain stops. In contrast, plants grown directly in the garden soil need much less attention. However, hand-watering will be needed in due course for those plants grown close to walls as in this situation the soil is likely to be drier than elsewhere in the garden, particularly if the wall faces away from the prevailing rain-bearing wind.

Plants short of moisture make very slow growth, look pale and spindly and will eventually wilt. Soil that is too wet over a long period is equally harmful because waterlogged soil lacks oxygen and discourages root activity. In extremes of both cases the leaves turn yellow and drop.

So far as container plants are concerned, it seems that more suffer from overwatering than from excessive dryness. Yet it is not difficult to strike the correct balance.

First, you must decide whether water is needed, which is not always evident from the appearance of the compost. A dry upper layer may conceal moist material beneath. If the plants are in clay pot or bowls, strike them gently with a suitable implement (the time-honoured and effective tool was a wooden cotton reel pushed on to the end of a cane). A ringing sound indicates dry compost; a dull note that it is moist. But check that the pot is not cracked, otherwise it will make a dull sound whatever the state of the compost.

For plastic pots the best method is to feel their weight. You will soon get to know the difference between a dry pot and one that contains moist compost.

Neither of these methods helps to determine the state of window boxes, tubs and other large containers. Until you become sufficiently experienced to know instinctively, the best you can do is to probe beneath the surface in an area where you will not damage plant roots. Alternatively, there are moisture meters available that will give an instant indication of the moisture content of the compost. Their behaviour is a little erratic, but with experience you will become more expert in their use.

The smaller the container the more quickly it will dry out and, whatever its size, this is particularly so when the plants are in full growth and the weather is hot and dry. In these conditions a daily check of the soil moisture should be made. Nevertheless, it is important not to water the plants at regu-

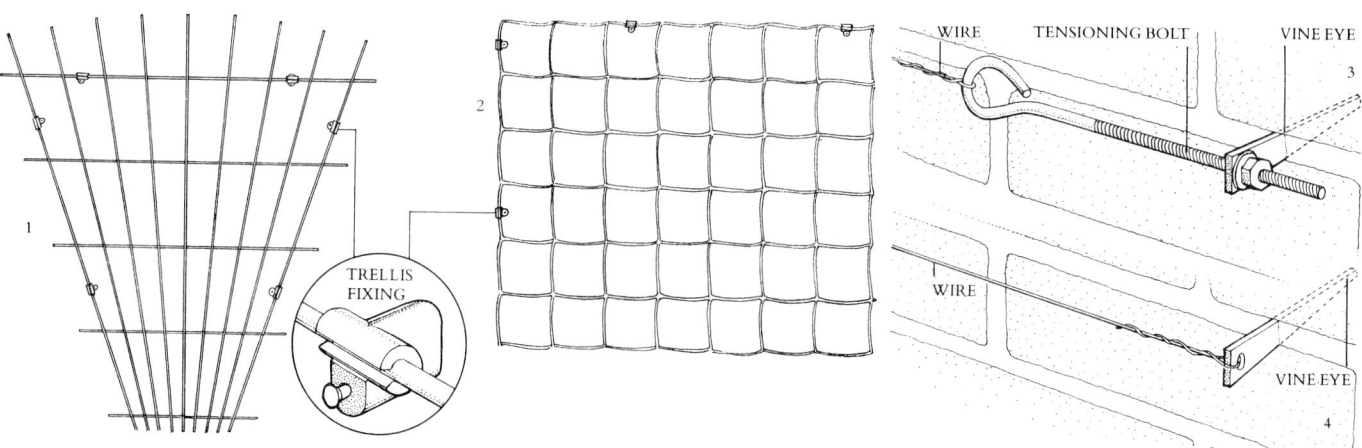

Alternatives to timber trellis are plastic-coated wire trellis (1), which is available in various designs, and plastic netting (2); special fixing blocks are usually supplied. A concealed means of support can be provided by tensioned wires fixed between vine eyes embedded in the wall. For heavy or large plants use tensioning bolts and heavy-gauge wire (3), otherwise simply twist around the eye by hand (4).

lar intervals regardless of conditions, for this is just how overwatering and subsequent waterlogging occurs.

Having decided that water is needed, always apply sufficient to get right down to the roots, not just enough to wet the surface. And, having done so, leave the plants until the compost starts to dry out and a fresh application is needed. Constant dribbling of small quantities does more harm than good.

Give young plants plenty of water before planting them out and then keep them well supplied for a few days afterwards. This is especially important if they were raised in a peat-based compost, which may remain as a dry, root-restricting patch unless properly wetted.

Use a watering can and direct the spout close to the compost, pouring gently so that the compost is not washed away. Fit a fine spray when watering seedlings or small plants. The best cans are those with low, long spouts that allow the most accurate control when watering; plastic ones are lighter than those made of metal.

If you need to use a hose in order to speed things up or because of the number of plants, you can either water directly from the open end or fit a trigger-type gun to provide on-off control, but do it gently and keep the pressure low.

In addition to watering, damping down helps to keep plants healthy and active during prolonged hot weather. This operation consists of spraying the plants, together with nearby paving and walls, to provide a more humid environment. Use either a can with a fine spray or one with a spray nozzle set to give a fine mist. Morning and early evening are the best times.

Automatic watering is possible, within limits, though it may be best to reserve this for holidays or long weekends away. It is asking a lot of any system to match the results obtained by careful observation of the plants.

One system consists of a bucket or plastic bag placed above the level of the plants and connected by pipelines to a number of adjustable drip nozzles. These may be positioned as needed and will keep the compost moist for as long

as the supply lasts. Depending on the system, containers hold up to about 5 gallons (22.5 litres) of water, but this will not last for many days during hot, dry weather.

An alternative, somewhat simpler system that is occasionally available, is provided by porous earthenware plugs. They are supplied by tubes led from an open-topped reservoir – any fairly shallow bowl or tank – placed at the same level as the containers. As the compost dries out, water is drawn along the tubes by capillary action, so the plants are able to dictate their own water needs.

There is also a range of plant containers with built-in self-watering. Each has a reservoir in the base that moistens the compost from the bottom upwards. An indicator shows when the reservoir needs refilling.

All these systems are particularly useful when you have to be away from home for a while – it is generally more realistic to ask a neighbour to refill a container every few days than to expect them to go around watering the plants individually.

Routine maintenance

Flowering can be prolonged by many weeks simply by removing flowers and flower spikes as they fade. This prevents the plant from setting seeds (which weakens it considerably) and encourages it to produce more blooms. If possible, make this a daily task during the main flowering season. Use a pair of secateurs or sharp scissors to nip off the flower stalk at its base.

While you are deadheading, keep an eye on the general condition of the plants – particularly for any signs of pests or diseases. Both are so much easier to control if caught in their very early stages. Keep some garden twine or plant ties handy to tie in new or straggling shoots of wall plants that are not self-supporting.

Container grown

Shrubs and roses need pruning to encourage the production of flowers or to

restrict growth in the same way as those grown in the open garden soil. You should follow the method appropriate to the variety concerned. Climbers, such as roses and clematis, can be trained to frame a window, cutting out or tying-in any side shoots growing in the wrong direction. Some shrubs and trees, pyracantha and laburnum are examples, can be pruned to go round a window in much the same way as fruit trees are trained to grow against a wall as an espalier or fan.

The container-grown shrubs may also require root pruning, otherwise their roots will come to occupy the whole container. This should be done every two or three years and will certainly help to restrict the size of the more vigorous varieties.

Take the entire plant and soil ball out of the container either in late autumn or spring and remove the outer soil and roots to a depth of 3–4in (8–10cm) from around the ball. Pack fresh compost round the outside when replacing it, and water to settle it in.

Shallow containers should be filled with fresh compost annually. It is impractical and unnecessary to repot large plants in deep pots and tubs, but you should remove the top layer of soil and replace it with fresh compost every spring. The very least you should do is to loosen the top layer of old compost and then gently fork in a dressing of general fertilizer.

The autumn, when you remove the hardy and half-hardy annuals that have finished their display, is a good time to examine your containers, particularly those made of wood, for any signs of damage or rot. Repair or replace if necessary, and apply wood preservative or oil-based paint – whichever was used before. Check that any plant supports are in good condition, particularly those used for wall shrubs and climbers, and critically examine the brackets and other fixtures that support heavy window boxes.

Feeding your plants

When planted in good-quality potting compost, whether based on loam or of

119

the soil-less type, young plants need no additional nourishment until they are well established and have made plenty of root growth. By this time the fertilizer content of the compost will be running low – especially in those based on peat – and supplementary feeding will be needed to maintain growth. But don't overdo it, especially at first, because too much is as bad as too little.

There is much to be said for liquid feeds, as these are immediately available to the plant's roots. Granular fertilizers have to dissolve first and it may be difficult to judge how long this is taking. Whatever kind you decide on, use a product formulated for plants grown in pots and other containers.

Foliar feeds – that is, liquid fertilizers sprayed on the leaves – are useful for plants that do not have a well-developed root system. They are quick-acting, but the results are short-lived.

Liquid feeding, following the instructions on the bottle or pack, should be sufficient to keep annuals and other short-term plants thriving. Obviously, fast-growing, vigorous plants, such as chrysanthemums, need more frequent and generous feeding than slow-grow-ing varieties, such as many rock plants.

Long-term plants – principally shrubs and climbers – need rather more solid nourishment. Hence the advice already given to replace some of the compost or add fertilizer.

Broadly, the foregoing feeding principles also apply to plants grown in the soil under walls. But granular feeds could replace liquid fertilizers because there is less risk of scorching the plants' roots. Alternatively apply an annual mulch of well-rotted farm manure in spring.

Pests and diseases

Strongly growing plants are less likely to suffer serious harm from either pests or diseases: it is the weaker that are at greatest risk. The other point to note is that prompt treatment is far more effective than leaving things until the trouble is well established.

Leading chemical manufacturers offer a wide range of products that kill most harmful insects and either prevent or check fungus diseases. In the case of pests, confine spraying to the affected plants rather than saturating everything.

Many pests, and the damage they cause, are easy to see and identify. Insects feasting on the sap of the shoot tips and on buds, are perhaps the commonest. Caterpillars are equally obvious, as to some extent are slugs. But sudden failure of a plant may also be due to invisible, underground pests such as leatherjackets and cutworms.

Diseases are better prevented than treated. So spray regularly against blackspot, mildew, etc., always following the manufacturer's instructions.

Disease is less likely to be a problem in a well-kept garden where dead plants are removed at once rather than left to rot. Soil pests thrive where there is decaying plant matter and other garden rubbish on which they can feed. Pots and other containers should be washed thoroughly between batches of plants, scrubbing earthenware and other containers with rough surfaces.

Tools and other aids

Remarkably little equipment is needed for window gardening. Watering cans and misters have been discussed earlier. So here are a few more basic aids, plus others which will make life easier.

A planting trowel comes in the former category, while a small hand fork is useful for loosening compacted soil and compost. For transplanting seedlings even smaller tools are available, but just as efficient would be an old, discarded kitchen spoon and fork. A spade or digging fork is necessary for cultivating the soil close to the house wall.

A trigger-type hand sprayer for dealing with pests and diseases will be sufficient for only a few plants. For larger plantings a small pump-up sprayer, with a metal lance attached to a plastic tube, is advisable.

A pair of secateurs is essential even if your garden is confined to just the small area around a window. But it is best not to be penny-pinching on quality, for a well-made pair of secateurs can last a lifetime.

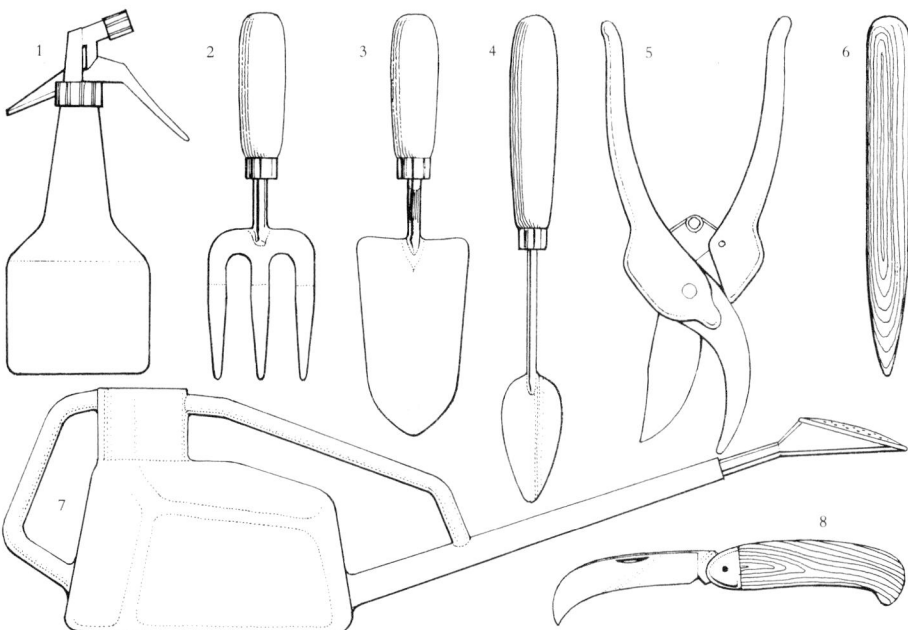

Window box and container gardening does not demand a large tool kit, but a few relatively inexpensive items are useful – trigger-type hand sprayer (1), hand fork (2), hand trowels (3,4), secateurs (5), dibber (6), watering can with fine spray (7), pocket- or pruning knife (8).

WINDOW PLANTS

Actinidia kolomikta KOLOMIKTA VINE A hardy twining deciduous climber usually reaching about 10ft(3m). Grown chiefly for its heart-shaped leaves which are suffused with pink at the tips, merging through white into dark green, often in three distinct zones. Plant in autumn or spring into rich loamy and well-drained soil at the foot of a wall; leaves colour best in full sun. Provide strong trellis support, and tie in leaders. Prune out old stems and cut to shape in early spring.

Agapanthus AFRICAN BLUE LILIES, LILY OF THE NILE Fleshy-rooted perennials with large, rounded, 6-12in(15-30cm), heads of 10-30 or more deep blue to white, funnel-shaped flowers borne in late summer and early autumn, on tall erect stems; leaves are strap-shaped, to 2ft(60cm) long, in dense clumps. Height: 2-3ft(60-90cm) as container plants. These plants actually thrive best when crowded in large tubs and containers; plant just below the soil surface, in mid-spring, setting them close; avoid root disturbance thereafter. Water freely in summer; deadhead after flowering. Containers should be moved under cover in cold areas in winter. *A. campanulatus* has soft blue flowers in flattish inflorescences. 'Isis' has deep blue flowers. *A.* 'Headbourne Hybrids' are the hardiest and most popular of the African blue lilies; evergreen and up to 2½ft(75cm) tall; they bear rounded, long-lasting flower clusters in shades of blue. *A. praecox orientalis* is evergreen and bears large spherical heads of numerous deep blue or white flowers.

Ageratum houstonianum (*A. mexicanum*) FLOSS FLOWER A half-hardy bushy annual with fluffy double flowers in 3-4in(8-10cm) clusters throughout summer; characteristically mid-blue in colour, but varieties come in shades of pale to deep blue, white or pinkish; leaves are heart-shaped and hairy. Height: 4-8in(10-20cm). Sow seed indoors in early spring; plant out early in summer in a sheltered sunny site.

Alyssum maritimum (*Lobularia maritima*) SWEET ALYSSUM A bushy and spreading dwarf hardy annual reaching just 4-6in(10-15cm) and invaluable for edging and carpeting window boxes and troughs. Profuse tiny white, lilac or purple flowers are borne in dense rounded clusters throughout the summer; leaves are narrow and greyish-green. Set out young seedlings in mid-spring in full sun.

Antirrhinum majus SNAPDRAGON A short-lived bushy perennial which is invariably cultivated as a half-hardy annual, with erect spikes of 'snapdragon' or 'dragon's-mouth' flowers (though hyacinth and penstemon-flowered strains also occur). Most colours are available, except blue; varieties are generally in mixed-colour strains. Sow seeds in early spring under glass; plant out in window boxes or pots in late spring to early summer in full sun or light shade to flower throughout summer and autumn. Pinch out tips to encourage bushy growth. Deadhead. Varieties are often listed in three groups according to height: *A. majus* Maximum varieties are the tallest, reaching 2½-4ft(0.75-1.2m) in height; Tetraploid varieties or tetra snaps (large ruffled flowers) include the Nanum varieties, 1-2ft(30-60cm) tall; and *A. majus* Pumilum (Nanum Compactum) varieties are dwarf, reaching 10in(25cm).

Arabis caucasica WALL or ROCK CRESS A hardy perennial, dwarf and often sprawling, but suitable for edging window boxes planted with spring bulbs. Evergreen foliage of hairy, grey-green, toothed leaves form clumps up to 8 in(20cm) high, studded from late spring to early summer with small, loose clusters of cross-shaped flowers, white or pink. Plant in autumn, in sun or light shade. Deadhead often and contain spread by cutting plants hard back after flowering. Named varieties are less invasive than the species and available as single or double forms, in white, lavender-pink and crimson.

Armeria THRIFT, SEA PINKS Hardy and neat perennials forming clumps of evergreen, greyish or green grass-like leaves. Flowers are small globes, up to 1in(2.5cm) wide, borne in late spring and summer. Thrifts make neat edgings for window boxes and other containers and also do well in shallow pots and troughs. Plant in autumn, in full sun, and remove flower stems as they fade. *A. caespitosa* grows only 2in(5cm) high, and the flowers, in shades of pink, almost smother the leaf mounds in late spring. *A. maritima* (sea pink) grows 8in(20cm) or more high, with pink, rose-red or white globular flowers on erect stems throughout summer.

Artemisia WORMWOODS, ANGELS-HAIR Hardy and half-hardy perennials and shrubs grown chiefly for their attractive foliage. Most are garden plants, but a few are outstanding as evergreen carpets and edgings in window boxes. The leaves are silvery and feathery, creating a perfect foil for brightly coloured flowers and for dark green miniature conifers. The small yellow button-like flowers in summer detract from the foliage and should be removed. Plant in spring, after frost, in a sunny and preferably sheltered position. *A. nitida* (*A. lanata*) is almost prostrate, to 1in(2.5cm) high, but spreading to 8in(20cm), with shiny, greyish foliage. *A. schmidtiana* 'Nana', up to 3in(8cm), forms dense cushions of bright silver and filigree leaves.

Aubrieta deltoidea FALSE ROCK CRESS A hardy evergreen perennial ideal for window boxes where the flower-studded stems can cascade over the edges. The hummocks of small, lightly hairy and grey-green leaves are hidden by four-petalled, cross-shaped flowers, up to ¾in(2cm) wide, from early spring on. In the species, the flowers are pink to pale lilac, but several varieties have larger blooms in deeper or paler shades of red and purple, and some have leaves variegated with gold or white. Height up to 4in(10cm) and wide-spreading, but easily curtailed by cutting the plants back hard as soon as flowering is finished. Plant in autumn or early spring, in good potting soil with a light sprinkling of lime, and in full sun.

Aucuba japonica JAPANESE AUCUBA

Hardy bushy evergreen shrub to 10ft(3m) in the open garden, but smaller as a tub plant. Leaves are glossy and laurel-like, 3-8in(8-20cm) long and widely toothed; they are particularly attractive in the variegated types like 'Maculata' ('Variegata', spotted laurel, gold-dust plant) with yellow-speckled leaves. Insignificant purplish flowers appear in spring, followed by persistent ½-⅝in(1-1.5cm) scarlet berries in clusters on female plants (a male must be planted nearby to effect pollination and fruit set). Plant in autumn or spring in large tubs, in any location. Tolerant of heavy shade and city pollution. If necessary, prune to shape in spring.

Begonia

Very showy, bushy plants with tuberous or fibrous roots and bright flowers and fleshy asymmetrical leaves. They are tender plants in temperate climates, but are popular for summer bedding in window boxes, tubs and hanging baskets. *B. semperflorens-cultorum* (wax begonias) includes several dwarf hybrids reaching 6-12in(15-30cm) high and usually grown as annuals in window boxes and pots. Profuse 1in(2.5cm) wide single flowers in shades of red, pink or white are borne in small panicles over a long period from midsummer to late autumn. Leaves are glossy green or bronze. Seed is sold as mixtures, as colour strains and as named varieties including F₁ hybrids. They can be sown under glass in early spring or bought as young seedlings. Plant out when all danger of frost is past, in light shade. *B. × tuberhybrida* (tuberous begonia) covers a group of tender, perennial, tuberous-rooted hybrids of complex parentage. Male and female flowers are borne separately on the same plant; the latter are insignificant compared with the showy, generally double, male flowers, up to

4in(10cm) across and borne in succession throughout summer and early autumn. Tubers, sold usually by colour, should be started into growth in late spring in boxes of peaty compost with the top of the tuber level with the surface. Moisten the compost (keeping the crowns of the tubers dry) and bring into growth in gentle heat. Move sprouted tubers to tubs and hanging baskets in summer, siting them in sun or light shade. Before the first frost, lift and dry off tubers before storing them in a frost-free place for the winter. The numerous named varieties are classified in groups according to flower shape and/or habit.

Bellis perennis ENGLISH DAISY

The true species is the familiar lawn daisy, but a number of garden varieties are superior, giving a succession of large single or double flowers in a range of pinks, reds and whites throughout spring and summer, and often into winter. They are hardy but short-lived perennials, best treated as biennials, with ¾-2in(2-5cm) wide flowers. Height 4-6in(10-15cm). Seeds can be sown in the garden or a cold frame, or seedlings bought in for spring bedding in window boxes, in sun or light shade. Deadhead to avoid self-seeding.

Berberis BARBERRIES

Mostly yellow-flowered, hardy and easily grown shrubs with attractive, often thorny leaves, and coloured berries. Leaves of deciduous species often acquire rich autumn colours. A few are suitable for container cultivation, planted in autumn or spring in full sun or light shade. Barberries are tolerant of dry conditions, making them particularly suitable for containers and for planting beneath windows, close to the wall. Prune to shape and to control spread; deciduous species in early spring, evergreens in summer. *B. × carminea* 'Bountiful' is deciduous, to 3ft(1m) tall, rich-flowering and with abundant coral-red fruits. *B. × irwinii* (*B. × stenophylla* 'Irwinii') is evergreen, to 3ft(1m) tall with deep yellow flowers. *B. panlanensis* has bright green, spiny evergreen leaves and is neat and compact enough for a window box. *B. ×*

stenophylla 'Corallina Compacta' is evergreen, to 1ft(30cm) tall, with narrow leaves, small yellow flowers opening from coral buds, and purple fruits. (Suitable for cultivation in quite small pots.) *B. thunbergii* is a compact shrub to 2ft(60cm) tall with brilliant autumn colours. It has several dwarf forms which grow well in large pots or small tubs.

Buxus BOX, BOXWOOD

Slow-growing, hardy evergreen shrubs with tiny glossy leathery leaves, often grown as low hedges. They respond well to formal topiary clipping and are suitable for tub and window box culture, especially welcome in winter. Plant in autumn or spring, in sun or partial shade and prune to desired shape in late summer. *B. microphylla* (little-leaf boxwood) is dense and rounded, to 3ft(1m), with thin and narrow leaves. *B. sempervirens* (common European box) eventually forms a small tree, but two dwarf varieties are excellent for larger window boxes and containers: 'Suffruticosa', a dwarf, slowly grows to 2ft(60cm), with bright green leaves (it may be clipped to maintain an even lower shrub), and 'Elegantissima' with silver-edged leaves is equally slow though eventually produces a larger dome unless pruned.

Calceolaria SLIPPER/POUCH FLOWERS

Bushy plants with showy, vividly coloured, pouched flowers and soft or hairy leaves. Usually grown as half-hardy perennials and much used in window boxes and pots in sheltered and sunny sites. Sow under glass, pot and then harden-off in a cold frame before planting out in good, preferably acid, potting compost. *C. × herbeohybrida* (florists' calceolaria) varieties grow to 8-12in(20-30cm) tall and have 1½-2½in(4-6cm) long flowers with a large inflated pouch, in shades of yellow, orange, red or brown, usually with distinct and contrasting spots or blotches. Seedlings can be raised under glass, for planting out in early summer. Discard after flowering, from midsummer to early autumn. *C. integrifolia* (bush calceolaria) is a half-hardy 1½-2ft(45-60cm) tall shrubby perennial and can be grown in large pots placed against sunny and sheltered walls. Bright yellow flowers, 1in(2.5cm) long, appear throughout summer; leaves are matt and wrinkled. Plant sturdy seedlings in early summer and pinch out shoot tips to encourage bushiness.

Callistephus chinensis CHINA ASTER, ANNUAL ASTER Popular half-hardy and easily grown annuals 8-30in(20-75cm) high for window box and pot cultivation, with single or double chrysanthemum-like, 3-5in(8-12cm) wide flowers in a wide range of colours (except yellows and oranges) in midsummer to autumn. Plant out seedlings in late spring, in sun or light shade, preferably sheltered from strong winds. Plants are prone to wilt disease and should be grown in fresh compost each year. Numerous varieties including dwarf types, to 1ft(30cm), are available, with new ones appearing yearly; most of these are wilt-resistant.

Camellia Slow-growing, generally hardy evergreen shrubs, valued for their beautiful late winter to mid-spring flowers. Though eventually reaching 10ft(3m) or more, camellias flower when quite small and many make excellent container plants. Flowers are white, pink or red and classified as single, semi-double, anemone-flowered, paeony-flowered, double and formal double. Varieties of *C. japonica* and *C. × williamsii* are the most suitable for growing in deep tubs of wood rather than concrete, which reacts adversely on these lime-haters. For the same reason choose a lime-free potting compost, with plenty of peat added. Plant in autumn, in sheltered west or north-facing positions, in light or partial shade (avoid east-facing positions where early morning sun may scorch frozen blooms); deadhead by hand after flowering. Little pruning is necessary and should be done after blooms have faded. Water thoroughly throughout the growing season, as drying-out results in bud drop. In cold areas move tubs under cover for the winter; elsewhere topdress with a winter mulch. *C. japonica* is bushy with glossy deep

green leaves to 4in(10cm) long, and 3-4in(8-10cm) wide flowers. *C. × williamsii* hybrids are very free-flowering and especially suitable for tub culture in northern gardens.

Campanula BELLFLOWERS Most of the bellflowers are invasive rock garden or border perennials, but a few make good subjects for edging window boxes and for hanging baskets. Generally hardy, they do equally well in sun or light shade; plant in autumn or spring and deadhead regularly to prevent self-seeding. Bellflowers, which are not too invasive for window boxes, include *C. arvatica*, 2in(5cm) with violet-blue or white starry flowers in midsummer; dwarf varieties of *C. carpatica*, especially 'Turbinata', 9in(23cm), with hairy grey foliage and blue cup-shaped flowers; the easily grown *C. cochlearifolia*, 4-6in(10-15cm), with blue or white ½in(1cm) bell flowers, throughout summer; the profuse and long-flowering *C. garganica*, to 6in(15cm), with blue and sometimes white-edged, starry flowers; and *C. pulla*, to 4in(10cm), with drooping violet-purple bells which do best in shade. For hanging baskets and to trail over edges of window boxes, there are the bright blue *C. portuschlagiana*, and *C. isophylla*. The latter is often grown as a house plant, but does well outdoors in summer; the trailing stems, which root where they touch the compost, are profusely studded with mid-blue starry flowers, 'Alba' is pure white. Move plants indoors before the first autumn frosts.

Campsis radicans AMERICAN TRUMPET CREEPER, TRUMPET VINE A generally hardy, deciduous, woody climber to 40ft(12m) if grown against a warm sheltered wall. It bears clusters of orange-red, 2-4in(5-10cm) long trumpet flowers in late summer; leaves are pinnate. Plant in autumn or spring, in deep, rich soil and full sun; provide support and tie in shoots until aerial roots develop and make the plant self-clinging. Winter-protect the roots for the first few years. Prune hard in early spring, cutting last year's lateral shoots back to a few buds at the base.

Canna × generalis (*C. × hybrida*) INDIAN SHOT Mostly tall, tender, rhizomatous-rooted plants used as 'dot plants' for tropical elegance in bedding schemes; a few dwarf varieties 1½-2½ft(45-75cm) in height are suitable for tubs and other deep containers. Flaring tubular flowers, to 4in(10cm) wide, appear in crowded spikes from summer to autumn; colours include red, pink, orange, yellow and white. The broad leaves are bright green, or bronze-purple on many red-flowering varieties. Plant 2-3in(5-7.5cm) deep in good peaty compost in spring, indoors, and move out only after danger of frost is past. Lift the plants as soon as flowering is over, dry off the rhizomes and overwinter them frost-free, in peat kept barely moist.

Ceanothus CALIFORNIAN LILACS Hardy deciduous and near-hardy evergreen flowering shrubs which actually give of their best when planted against sunny walls, in open ground or in tall pots and deep tubs. Most flower in late spring and early summer when the shrubs become a haze of blue from the dense flower clusters. Plant deciduous species in early autumn, evergreens in mid-spring, in deep pots of good potting compost or in well-drained soil, neutral or slightly acid. The best position is against a sheltered south- or west-facing wall; provide trellis support in the early years to train the shrubs in the desired direction. If necessary, prune to shape after flowering. *C. × burkwoodii* is evergreen, up to 8ft(2.4m) and hardy in most temperate areas; it is summer-flowering, carrying its bright blue flowers from midsummer until early autumn. *C. dentatus* is also evergreen, but needs more shelter; the small rounded leaves are shiny bright green in the variety 'Russellianus', which flowers in early summer with blue, rounded clusters. *C. ×* 'Gloire de Versailles' is deciduous, hardy and vigorous but suitable for container cultivation as it responds well to hard spring pruning; the soft blue, scented 8in(20cm) long flower clusters appear throughout summer. *C. ×* 'Topaz' is similar, but smaller in all respects.

Centaurea *C. rutifolia* (*C.cineraria candidissima*) is a silvery-white-leaved perennial reaching 18in(45cm) in height, chiefly grown as a foliage plant; though moderately hardy, it is best propagated each year by cuttings taken in early autumn, overwintered under glass and planted out in spring. It is best as a tub plant, in full sun; the leaves are deeply dissected and provide an excellent foil for other plants. Dwarf and compact forms, to 1ft(30cm), of the hardy annual cornflower, *C. cyanus*, are suitable for window boxes; they bear sprays of 1in(2.5cm) flowers in a range of colours above grey-green leaves throughout summer. *C. gymnocarpa* (dusty miller) is another foliage plant with deeply cut leaves, thickly felted with white hairs. It is a shrubby, semi-hardy perennial, up to 2ft(60cm) high and should be treated like *C. rutifolia*.

Chaenomeles FLOWERING QUINCES, CYDONIA Stout-branched, spiny, deciduous shrubs of spreading habit 6ft(1.8m) or more in height, best grown against a wall of any aspect and trained against trellis. Showy saucer-shaped flowers, to 1½in(4cm) wide, appear in clusters, from early spring or even late winter in milder climates; they resemble single wild roses and bloom on naked stems before leaves expand. Apple- or pear-shaped yellow fruits ripen in late summer to autumn. Plant in autumn or spring in good loamy soil. Prune to shape after flowering, removing crossing branches and shortening all side-shoots. *C. japonica* is a low-growing shrub, suitable for planting beneath windows. It seldom reaches more than 3ft(90cm) in height and bears orange-red apple-blossom flowers in late spring. 'Alpina' is smaller still, with brick-red flowers, followed in autumn by scented, yellow fruits. *C. speciosa* (japonica, Japanese quince) has red flowers often up to 2½in(6cm) wide, followed by saw-toothed glossy leaves to 3in(8cm) long. There are numerous varieties with flowers ranging from crimson through pink to white.

Chamaecyparis FALSE CYPRESSES Very hardy evergreen conifers with flattened sprays of fine, scaly foliage, generally of conical or columnar shape. The species are tall trees, but a number of very slow-growing dwarf varieties are suitable for specimen planting in tubs and containers and even window boxes. Plant in autumn in good compost, adequately drained, and site in sun or light shade; coloured-leaved forms are best in full sun. Dwarf varieties of *C. lawsoniana* (Lawson's cypress), *C. obtusa* and *C. pisifera* can all be grown in tubs or window boxes.

Cheiranthus WALLFLOWER Very popular hardy biennials for spring and early summer colour. Flowers are up to 1in(2.5cm) across in spikes of various colours; leaves are lance-shaped and plants are of bushy habit. Raised from seeds in the open garden or purchased as young plants in autumn ready to plant out in autumn in window boxes and troughs, 10-12in(25-30cm) apart, preferably in a sunny position. To encourage bushy growth the growing tip and taproot should be pinched out when transplanted. Good plants may be propagated from cuttings. *C. cheiri* is the common English wallflower which is represented in cultivation by a large number of named varieties covering a range of colours from yellow through to deep crimson. Dwarf varieties (8-12in[20-30cm]) are particularly useful for window boxes. *C.* × *allionii* (Siberian wallflower; correctly listed as *Erysimum* × *allionii*), height 15in(38cm) bears loose globular heads of smaller flowers; the colour range is limited to yellows and oranges.

Chionodoxa luciliae GLORY OF THE SNOW An early-flowering, hardy dwarf bulb suitable for window boxes and for underplanting deciduous wall shrubs. Starry, blue flowers with a white eye appear in small clusters on 3-6in(8-15cm) stems; leaves are narrowly strap-shaped. Plant bulbs 3in(8cm) deep in autumn in a sunny or partially shaded site. 'Alba' has white flowers; 'Rosea' has lilac-pink flowers.

Choisya ternata MEXICAN ORANGE An evergreen shrub, native to Mexico, which in cool climates succeeds best against a wall. It is suitable for growing in tall pots and large tubs placed in a sheltered position. In such a confined space it grows up to 6ft(1.8m), slightly more in open ground. The deep green leaves have a glossy sheen; the sweetly fragrant, pure white flowers appear in flat, wide clusters from late spring onwards. Plant in spring, in deep containers of potting compost, or in the open in any type of well-drained soil, in a sunny site sheltered from winds. Pruning is rarely necessary, but cut back frost-damaged shoots to their base in spring.

Chrysanthemum This large and popular plant group ranges from tiny alpines to huge hothouse perennials. Between these two extremes are numerous annuals and perennials, several of which are ideal for containers of all kinds. Annual chrysanthemums include the marguerite (*C. frutescens*), correctly a shrubby perennial but usually raised in quantity as annuals for window boxes, pots and hanging baskets. It grows 12-18in(30-45cm) high with elegant, thin but wiry stems bearing pale green leaves and white or yellow daisy-like flowers, 2in(5cm) wide, for most of the summer; it makes a marvellous foil for fuchsias. Other annual types suitable for window boxes and pots are *C. multicaule*, up to 1ft(30cm) tall, with simple, golden, daisy-like flowers in late summer; and the pompon varieties, 10-12in(25-30cm) tall, of *C. parthenium,* which come in white, yellow and gold. These can be raised from autumn or spring seedlings, but marguerites must be increased from cuttings in autumn. The hardy perennial Shasta daisies (*C. maximum*) are generally too large, up to 3ft(90cm) tall, for window boxes, but several, including 'Esther Read', a double white, do well in pots and similar containers. Cut stems back to the crown in late autumn. Outdoor varieties of the so-called florists' chrysanthemum are mainly too tall for pot cultivation, though pompon and spray varieties are suitable for window boxes in sheltered sites. Specially dwarfed varieties of the florists' chrysanthemum bring welcome colour to autumn boxes, though expensive to buy for massed displays; they do not retain their dwarf habit for a second year and should be planted out in the garden.

Cineraria cruenta (*Senecio cruentus*) CINERARIA A tender perennial, usually cultivated as a greenhouse or indoor biennial. Some varieties are suitable for summer bedding in window boxes provided these are sheltered from hot sun and strong winds. Colourful daisy flowers ¾-3in(2-8cm) wide are borne in broad clusters in shades of pink, carmine, purple and blue, often with white zoning. Seeds can be sown in a cool greenhouse in summer and overwintered in gentle heat; in practice it is easier to purchase young plants in early summer. Various mixed-colour selections are available; the most suitable for window boxes are the double-flowered, height 1-1½ft(30-45cm), with fully- or semi-double flowers; and the compact Multiflora Nana varieties, height 12-15in(30-38cm), with broad-petalled single flowers. Discard after flowering.

Citrus mitis CALAMONDIN Several species of the evergreen citrus group can be grown as greenhouse or house plants; only in Mediterranean-type climates are they hardy. They are attractive in terracotta pots and may be stood outside for the summer months and moved indoors before autumn. The calamondin is one of the best citrus for pot cultivation, growing to about 18in(45cm) high. Small, 1in(2.5cm), star-shaped, fragrant flowers appear during spring and early summer; the orange-yellow bitter fruits are unlikely to ripen outdoors. Leaves are lance-shaped and glossy dark green. Stand in a sunny sheltered spot. Topdress with compost rather than repot.

Clematis These are among the most popular of hardy woody climbers, suitable for training up walls and fences, around windows and over porches. They grow to 8-15ft(2.5-4.5m) or more according to species/variety and can be grown in beds at the foot of a wall or in deep tubs and trained on trellis or plastic mesh. Flowers may be cup or bell-shaped, pendent or opened-out flat from a central tuft of stamens. Leaves are entire or pinnate and have twining stalks by which the plants cling. Plant in autumn or spring in well-prepared deep acid or alkaline soil against walls of any aspect. The roots must be kept cool and shaded from direct sun, either by means of paving or by a vegetative ground cover. *C. armandii* is evergreen and somewhat tender, needing a warm and sheltered wall. The white, saucer-shaped flowers appear in mid-spring amid the glossy foliage. Prune lightly to shape if necessary, after flowering. *C. macropetala*, deciduous, has semi-double, 2-3in(5.8cm) violet-blue, pendent bell flowers in late spring to early summer. Prune as *C. armandii*. *C. montana* is an extremely vigorous deciduous climber, with profuse 2in(5cm) white flowers in late spring to early summer. Excellent for a north-facing position. 'Elizabeth' and 'Rubens' have rosy-pink flowers, the latter among bronze-purple leaves. Prune to restrain growth after flowering. *C. orientalis* has nodding bell-shaped, 1-2in(2.5-5cm) flowers, orange-yellow and fragrant in late summer followed by showy, silky seed-heads in autumn. *C. tangutica* is rather similar with lantern-shaped flowers. Both have fern-like deciduous foliage. Prune in late winter/early spring. *C. viticella* is a profuse-flowering deciduous species. Consult a specialist catalogue for numerous varieties and large-flowered clematis hybrids.

Cobaea scandens CUP-AND-SAUCER VINE, CATHEDRAL/MONASTERY BELLS A half-hardy vigorous climber which, when grown outdoors, is treated as an annual. It grows to 15ft(4.5m), though generally less in temperate areas. Its pendulous, violet and green, bell-shaped flowers with a prominent green calyx are up to 3in(8cm) long, and appear on long stalks in summer and autumn. Leaves are dark green and pinnate, the terminal leaflet being replaced by a long tendril. Plant out seedlings after danger of frost is past, in ordinary soil (rich soil encourages excessive leaf growth at the expense of flowers) or in deep pots placed beneath a window with sun and shelter. Plants require support, such as trellis or wires, and may be trained around a window. 'Alba' has white flowers.

Coleus blumei FLAME NETTLE In cultivation this species is represented by numerous hybrids, sometimes listed as *C. × hybridus*. Reaching 8-24in(20-60cm) in height, they are spectacularly coloured foliage plants with nettle-like, 1½-6in(4-15cm) long leaves in variegated shades of green, yellow, bronze, red, pink, white and purple. They are tender sub-shrubby perennials, but usually treated as early sown half-hardy annuals, and are suitable for window boxes and pots and as centre plants in hanging baskets, though rain and strong winds may spoil the foliage; they need sun and shelter. The narrow spikes of blue and white flowers should be pinched out as soon as they appear to prevent 'bolting'. Plant outdoors after last frosts and feed weekly with a liquid fertilizer. Hybrids are usually sold as mixtures. Flame nettles are best discarded at the end of the season, after tip cuttings have been taken, which root easily in water.

Convolvulus tricolor (*C. minor*) DWARF MORNING GLORY A half-hardy bushy annual 8-12in(20-30cm) high, with profuse but often transient, trumpet-shaped flowers in shades of blue or red, that bloom from midsummer on in the upper leaf axils; leaves are dark green and variously shaped. They do well in window boxes and tubs, with seedlings planted out in late spring. Deadhead to encourage continuous flowering. Varieties are available in shades of blue, violet and pure white, usually with yellow or white centres.

Cordyline CABBAGE PALM, DRACAENA These evergreen shrubs are tender in temperate climates, but a few species are frequently used as summer bedding plants. In elegant tubs, placed by windows and doorways, their rosettes of narrow, arching leaves add a touch of the exotic. *C. australis* (*Dracaena indivisa*, giant dracaena, grass palm) is one

125

of the hardiest species. In cold areas it can be planted out in early summer when all danger of frost is past and must be moved indoors or to a greenhouse before autumn. However, in sheltered areas, it can be left out all winter. As a container plant, in sun or light shade, it grows up to 3ft(90cm) high and is fairly wind-resistant; the narrow, sword-shaped, greenish-grey leaves grow in a large tuft from the top of a short, palm-like trunk. *C. indivisa* grows to the same height in a tub but differs in having wider mid-green leaves, with red or yellow midribs.

Cotoneaster Among the best of the hardy berrying shrubs, cotoneasters range from prostrate to bushy and arching types, deciduous or evergreen species. Some can be trained against walls (planted either in open ground or in tall pots), others are dwarf enough for window boxes and small pots. Flowers are small, ⅓-½in(8-12mm), white or pinkish, followed by bright red, yellow or black berries in autumn to early winter. Plant in autumn or late winter in a sunny position, in ordinary soil in open ground or in good potting compost in containers. Pruning is rarely necessary, but stray shoots may be trimmed back to shape – deciduous types in late winter, evergreens in mid-spring. *C. conspicuus* 'Decorus' is low-growing, to 3ft(90cm), with small, dark evergreen leaves and bright red berries. Good wall plant in open ground. *C. horizontalis* is one of the most popular shrubs for planting near house windows and will do well in tall pots. Average height 2-3ft(60-90cm). Small, rounded, dark green deciduous leaves are borne on characteristic her-ringbone branches and turn brilliant red in autumn. The red berries often persist until spring. 'Variegatus' has creamy-white edged leaves with pinkish tints in autumn. *C. microphyllus cochleatus* (small-leaved cotoneaster) has tiny dark, glossy evergreen leaves and scar-let berries on near-prostrate stems. Ideal for window boxes or trailing from small half-pots.

Crocus Among the most popular and colourful hardy dwarf bulbs (corms), mostly flowering in late winter and early spring. Generally 3-4in(8-10cm) tall. Flowers are upright and goblet-shaped, often opening starry or cup-shaped with or just before the narrow, grassy leaves. Plant 3-4in(8-10cm) deep in early autumn in a sunny position, in shallow pots and containers or massed in window boxes, on their own or in association with dwarf evergreen shrubs and primroses. *C. chrysanthus* has large flowers, up to 3in(8cm) high, in late winter and early spring. Numer-ous varieties are available with bi-coloured flowers coloured yellow, pur-ple, soft blue and bronze. *C. sieberi* is pale mauve with a yellow throat, from early spring. *C. speciosus* is an autumn-flowering crocus, up to 5in(12cm) high, with bright blue goblet flowers show-ing prominent orange stigmas. *C. ver-nus* is the parent of the popular Dutch crocuses with colours ranging from white through silvery blue to violet. These bear large flowers with a height of up to 5in(12cm) in spring.

Cyclamen SHOOTING STAR Several hardy relatives of the winter-flowering florists' cyclamen are suitable for grow-ing in window boxes. They are tuber-ous plants, characterized by their rounded, often mottled leaves and backswept, shuttlecock flowers. Plant corms 2in(5cm) deep (smooth domed side downwards) in peaty compost in a partially shaded, sheltered spot in late summer or early autumn. *C. coum* flowers from late winter through to spring, with broad-petalled, carmine-pink blooms on 3in(8cm) stems. *C. pur-purascens* (*C. europaeum*) is summer to autumn-flowering, deep carmine and sweetly scented; 4in(10cm) tall. *C. hederifolium* (*C. neapolitanum*), 4in(10cm) high, flowers freely, above green and silvery leaves, long into au-tumn; colours vary from white to pale pink, crimson and magenta.

Cytisus × racemosus FLORISTS' BROOM An evergreen 1½ft(45cm) tall or more shrub, often grown as a pot plant, but ideal for adding a splash of colour to a window box or container. Small grey-green leaves make a good foil to the vivid yellow, fragrant pea-flowers which appear in profuse clusters throughout spring to early summer. Plant in early spring into ordinary soil in full sun (rich soil will promote leaf growth at the expense of flowering). Overwinter indoors in colder areas.

Dahlia × cultorum DWARF BEDDING DAHLIAS Like their taller relatives these plants bear showy, colourful flowers, but are lower growing, about 12-20in (30-50cm) high, and are more compact. Bedding dahlias are annuals, half-hardy in temperate climates, and should be discarded at the end of the season. The flowers bloom from midsummer to autumn, are 1-4in(2.5-10cm) wide, single, semi-double or double in shades of yellow, orange, pink, red, lilac and white. Leaves are rounded and rich green or lightly bronzed. Plant sturdy seedlings when all danger of frost is past, in window boxes, tubs or pots in full sun. Water thoroughly, daily throughout summer, but do not apply fertilizers as these encourage excessive leaf growth. Deadhead regularly.

Dianthus CARNATIONS AND PINKS Perennial, annual and biennial cottage garden plants, many with a charming fragrance and delicate- or brightly coloured flowers in shades of pink, red, mauve and white. The narrow, grey-green leaves are evergreen in perennial species, and rise from tufted crowns. The modern border or cut-flower carnations look out of place in contain-ers, but the true species, annual, bien-nial and perennial, look charming in window boxes and as edging in tubs and large pots. Set out seedlings of annuals in spring, biennials and peren-nials in autumn, in ordinary neutral pot-ting compost, and in full sun. Deadhead regularly. *D. barbatus* (sweet William) is a hardy biennial, 6-24in(15-60cm) high with flattened or domed 3-5in (8-12cm) wide clusters of variously col-oured or bicoloured flowers borne on sturdy erect stems in early summer. Dwarf varieties are particularly suitable for window boxes. *D. chinensis* (Indian pink) is a mid- to late-summer-flowering annual, 6-12in(15-30cm) high with single 1-2in(2.5-5cm), frilled flowers; sold as bedding mixtures or as single colours. *D. deltoides* (maiden pink) is a mat-forming perennial, 6-10in(15-25cm) high, covered throughout summer with ½-¾in(1-2cm) wide flowers in various shades of pink, red and white. It forms neat hummocks and will thrive in shallow containers. *D. neglectus* (glacier pink) is a cushion-like perennial, 4-8in(10-20cm) high with 1¼in(3cm) pink or crimson flowers in mid- and late summer. Garden pinks are all hybrids, growing 10-15in(25-37cm) high; the so-called modern pinks have a longer flowering period than old-fashioned pinks, but though perennial are short-lived. The ruffled flowers are self or bicoloured, white, pink, red and mauve, single or double, 1-2in(2.5-5cm) wide and usually sweetly fragrant. Modern pinks are ideal for tub and pot culture, and dwarf varieties for window boxes. Numerous named varieties are available and specialist catalogues should be consulted.

Eccremocarpus scaber CHILEAN GLORY FLOWER VINE Semi-woody, evergreen fast-growing climber, to 10-15ft(3-4.5m), with 1in(2.5cm) long scarlet to yellow tubular flowers in racemes during summer and autumn. It is useful for training on a warm sheltered wall, but except in mild areas is generally cut to the ground each winter by frosts. It will usually spring again from the roots if these are given protection. Alternatively treat the plant as a half-hardy annual, raising it from seed sown under glass in late winter and planted at the base of a sunny wall, in loamy, well-drained soil in late spring. Provide support with wire or trellis; shoots cling by tendrils.

Elaeagnus pungens OLEASTER, THORNY ELAEAGNUS A hardy evergreen foliage shrub of vigorous growth, much used for hedges. Usually fast-growing, the species has produced one slow-growing variety, 'Maculata', which is useful in containers. As a mature shrub in a deep pot or tub it eventually reaches 5ft(1.5m), and as a young plant it will succeed for several years in a window box. It thrives happily in

shade, where the ovate and leathery leaves, heavily splashed with gold, add brightness to the dullest winter scene. Plant in spring or early autumn, in shade or sun. Pruning is rarely needed, but any shoots with all-green leaves should be cut out entirely.

Erica HEATHS A large group of evergreen flowering shrubs, ranging from near prostrate to more than 20ft(6m). The majority are lime-haters, but the winter- and spring-flowering species and cultivars, ideal for window boxes, are less fussy about soil and can be planted in ordinary potting compost. All heaths are characterized by their spikes of bell-shaped flowers borne above and among the needle-like foliage. The flowers persist for a long period and are attractive even as they fade. Plant in autumn or spring, in full sun. After flowering, shear over the shrubs to remove faded flower stems and keep the hummocks neat. The white or purple-pink winter-flowering heaths offered for sale by florists around Christmas are tender; they must be grown indoors and are not suitable for window box cultivation, unlike the hardy *E. carnea* (*E. herbacea*) and its numerous varieties. These grow 2-12in(5-30cm) high and bear terminal flower spikes from late autumn right through to late spring, in white and shades of pink. Leaves are usually bright green, but golden and bronze forms are often available. For deeper and larger boxes, taller heaths like *E.* × *darleyensis* make a colourful display throughout winter. Up to 2ft(60cm) high, the 6in(15cm) long spikes of bell flowers, in shades of white, pink and rosy-red, begin to appear around Christmas and continue until late spring.

Erysimum ALPINE WALLFLOWER Hardy herbaceous perennials, related to the biennial wallflower (*Cheiranthus*) and bearing dark greyish green foliage and typical, if smaller, flower clusters, sweetly scented. They are useful in window boxes, interplanted with late tulips, where they can continue the display well into summer. Easily grown,

they thrive in any kind of compost, but flower best in full sun; plant in autumn. *E. alpinum* (*Cheiranthus alpinus*) grows only 6in(15cm) high, with bright yellow flowers; named varieties are taller, with pale yellow or mauve flowers. *E. capitatum* (*Cheiranthus capitatus*), up to 10in(25cm), has the largest flower clusters, each bloom 1in(2.5cm) wide and creamy-yellow from late spring onwards.

Euonymus SPINDLES, SPINDLE BERRIES Hardy deciduous and evergreen shrubs grown for their foliage. Most are vigorous plants more suitable as wall shrubs than for containers, though a few can be confined to deep tubs and window boxes without any harm. Plant in autumn or spring in any location, though variegated forms colour best in sun. *E. fortunei radicans* (*E. radicans*) makes an admirable wall shrub with its dark, glossy-green evergreen, 1-2in(2.5-5cm) leaves, and clusters of orange-red fruits in autumn following insignificant whitish flowers in early summer. Plant in autumn, in good garden soil, and against a sheltered wall. The following varieties are outstanding when planted in a sunny position: 'Emerald Gaiety' (rounded leaves, edged white); and 'Silver Queen' or 'Variegatus' (broad leaves, edged white), suitable for a window box where it will maintain a height of up to 1ft(30cm) for several years. *E. japonicus* itself is unsuitable for container culture, but several of its evergreen varieties are slow growing and dense enough for tubs and deep pots: 'Microphyllus' (dainty, glossy green small leaves); 'Microphyllus Pulchellus', with golden variegations; and 'Microphyllus Variegatus', silver-white edges to the leaves.

Fatsia japonica FALSE CASTOR-OIL PLANT A moderately hardy, evergreen suckering shrub of rather confused nomenclature, often called the castor-oil plant which truly belongs to an unrelated species. Sometimes it is listed as *Aralia sieboldii* or *A. japonica*. Grown for its very large and leathery, lobed or hand-like leaves up to 1ft(30cm) across, this plant reaches 7ft(2m) with age, but may be kept in a container until too large; the leaves are generally smaller on young plants. The variety 'Moseri' has larger leaves but makes a more compact plant; 'Variegata' has whitish margined leaves. The flowers are small and creamy-white but come in branched heads of pompon-like clusters. Propagate by semi-ripe cuttings or by suckers; plant in autumn or spring in a sheltered, semi-shaded position.

Forsythia GOLDEN BELLS These hardy deciduous common shrubs are often seen as overgrown and leggy specimens through neglect following their magnificent golden-yellow, massed flower display in spring. Several species, and in particular *F. suspensa*, are excellent as container shrubs in pots and tubs or trained against walls of any aspect including north. In pots, they can be trained as standard trees as they respond well to hard pruning, and on walls they are easily kept within bounds. *F. suspensa* grows 10ft(3m) high, more as a wall shrub, and has mid-green leaves; in early and mid-spring the leafless branches are clothed along their entire length with small clusters of deep yellow flowers, each 1in(2.5cm) across. This, and other species, flowers on shoots made in the previous year; to ensure the annual floral display, prune hard as soon as flowering is over. Plant in autumn, in large pots of good potting compost, or at the foot of walls in any kind of garden soil.

Fuchsia Popular though often somewhat tender shrubs grown for their profuse characteristic nodding flowers and neat foliage. Leaves are generally to 2in(5cm) long and deciduous unless grown in frost-free conditions. Most fuchsias are bushy, reaching 2-4ft(0.6-1.2m) or more, or may be pruned and trained as standards (suitable for the centre of large tubs); some varieties are semi-prostrate and suitable for hanging baskets; others are dwarf and compact, making excellent pot and window box plants. Tender varieties must be given protection overwinter; hardier varieties may be grown outdoors all year, but will often be cut to the ground by frosts. Propagate by softwood cuttings rooted

in a cold frame in summer; plant in fertile soil in full sun or partial shade; pinch leaders to encourage bushiness. *F. × hybrida* includes a profusion of showy large-flowered hybrids, some tender, others moderately hardy. Sepals and petals are frequently of contrasting colours, ranging from white, through pinks, reds, mauves and deep purples. Flowers are borne in succession throughout summer and early autumn. *F. magellanica* is deciduous, quite hardy and may form a quite large plant, to 8ft(2.5m) in mild areas, but if pruned is ideal for larger containers. Leaves are smaller than above and young stems are slender and reddish. Flowers are small and narrow with bright red sepals and violet-purple petals. Varieties include *gracilis* 'Variegata' (grown for its attractive creamy-yellow, pink-flushed leaf margins, as well as for its flowers), and *gracilis* 'Versicolor' (leaves grey-green edged creamy-white, flushed crimson when young).

Galanthus nivalis SNOWDROP An ultra-hardy late winter- to early spring-flowering 4-8in(10-20cm) tall bulb. Flowers are solitary, nodding, ¾-1¼in(2-3cm) long, bell-shaped with green-tipped inner and pure white outer petals; leaves are narrow, strap-shaped and slightly glaucous. Plant bulbs 4in(10cm) deep in small groups (best transplanted in spring while growing) in rich soil in partial shade. Varieties include the hybrid with *G. plicatus* called 'Atkinsii' (large flowers, very early) and 'Plena' (double).

Gazania Herbaceous perennials which in temperate climates are killed by frost and therefore treated as half-hardy annuals; the exotic, brilliantly coloured flowers persist from midsummer until autumn frost. Excellent for window boxes and pots, provided they are in full sun. Most gazanias are hybrids (*G. × hybrida*), growing about 10in(25cm) high, with dark greyish-green narrow leaves. The flowers, which close in the evening and in dull weather, come in a range of bright colours including yellow, tangerine, orange, red, pink, scarlet and bronze, frequently in bicolours

or strikingly marked with contrasting zones. Strains are chiefly available in mixed colours ('Monarch' and 'Sunshine'). Set out seedlings in early summer when all danger of cold nights is past; discard in autumn or move pots to a cool greenhouse for overwintering.

Godetia grandiflora SATIN FLOWER Hardy annuals and among the easiest and most successful plants for containers, carrying their bright funnel-shaped white, pink or crimson flowers from early summer until autumn. Varieties come in single or mixed colours, usually listed according to flower shape, such as Azalea-flowered types, with 2in(5cm) wide semi-double and many-petalled flowers. Sturdy and compact, with bright green pointed leaves, the dwarf varieties, 12-15in(30-38cm) high, become veritable carpets of colour if planted in full sun. Set out seedlings in spring in not too-rich compost or foliage will be produced at the expense of flowers. Dwarf verbenas make good companions.

Gypsophila elegans BABY'S BREATH A hardy, easily grown annual, ideal for window boxes in summer to early autumn when the dainty, loose white, pale pink or rosy-carmine flower sprays appear. Leaves are glaucous-green, thin and narrow, set in pairs on the wiry stems. Plant out seedlings in spring, in a sunny site; remove plants at the end of the season. Dwarf varieties, 8-12in(20-30cm) high, are ideal for containers.

Hebe SHRUBBY VERONICAS Moderately hardy evergreen shrubs grown both for their foliage and flowers. Most species reach 3-5ft(1-1.5m) or more with age, but young plants and dwarf or prostrate types are suitable for window containers. Flowers are normally tiny with fluffy stamens, borne in long and tapering, or rounded spikes, in shades of mauve, purple/blue, reddish-mauve, pink or white. Leaves are mostly leathery, though in some species are tiny and scale-like ('whipcord'). Propagate by semi-ripe or hardwood cuttings; plant in autumn or spring in a sunny and preferably sheltered position. *H.* × *andersonii* 'Variegata' has fleshy, 4in(10cm), grey-green leaves with creamy-white edging and mottling. Flowers are lavender-blue fading whitish in long racemes in late summer. *H.* × *a.* 'Midsummer Beauty' has very profuse 5in(12cm) racemes of lavender-purple flowers. *H.* × 'Autumn Glory' has dark green leaves and violet flowers from summer to winter. *H.* × 'Carl Teschner' makes a spreading mound to about 8in(20cm) and becomes smothered with brilliant violet-blue flowers during the summer. *H.* × *franciscana* 'Blue Gem' is a compact and dome-shaped hybrid with rounded glossy green leaves and squat 2-3in(5-8cm) racemes of violet-blue flowers throughout summer and autumn. *H.* × 'Margery Fish' is compact with leaves bronzed in winter; violet-blue and white flowers. *H. pinguifolia* has a spreading habit, reaching 6-12in(15-30cm), and makes mats of grey-green leaves and has white flowers; its variety 'Pagei' has bluer leaves. Garden hybrids derived from *H. speciosa* have profuse flowers in summer and autumn; these include 'Alicia Amherst' (deep violet) and 'La Seduisante' (4in[10cm] racemes of magenta-mauve flowers).

Hedera IVIES Vigorous evergreen, woody-stemmed and self-supporting climbers reaching up to 30ft(9m), popular for providing a dense covering of dark green or often variegated foliage over walls and around windows, or as a ground cover. Many small-leaved varieties are suitable for planting in containers, but must be pruned when they become too large. Two types of leaves are produced: juvenile, often attractively lobed, and adult, non-climbing stems with simple leaves and bearing the somewhat insignificant globular clusters of greenish flowers which later develop poisonous berries (typically black). Ivy grows well in any soil and aspect, being tolerant of quite heavy shade (except coloured-leaved forms). The climbing stems are self-supporting on brickwork, etc. (often considered damaging to old mortar). Propagate by semi-ripe or hardwood cuttings of juvenile shoots. Plant be-

tween autumn and spring, during fine weather. *H. canariensis* (Canary Island ivy) is less hardy than most, but bears large leaves, sometimes up to 8in(20cm) long. 'Gloire de Marengo' ('Variegata') is very popular, with silver-grey and cream-edged leaves. *H. colchica* (Persian ivy) has larger heart-shaped leaves to 10in(25cm) long. Varieties include 'Dentata' (elephant's ear ivy, paler green, toothed leaves); 'Sulphur Heart' ('Paddy's Pride', splashed yellow); and 'Dentata Variegata' ('Variegata', like 'Dentata', but edged cream). *H. helix* (common ivy) is represented by numerous varieties, mostly with smaller leaves than above, including: 'Buttercup' (small gold-yellow leaves turning yellow-green with age); 'Deltoidea' ('Sweetheart') (heart-shaped leaves); 'Glacier' (greyish, edged cream); 'Goldheart' (small dark green leaves with a yellow central blotch); 'Little Diamond' (small, diamond-shaped, white-variegated leaves); and 'Sagittifolia' (arrow-shaped leaves).

Helianthemum alpestre SUN ROSE, ROCK ROSE Hardy evergreen shrublet, suitable for creeping over the edges of permanent window boxes and tubs. It is less invasive than other rock roses, and trimming after flowering contains its spread and often induces a second show of bloom in autumn. It grows 3in(8cm) high, with mid-green elliptic leaves along the wiry stems. In midsummer these are hidden by a carpet of saucer-shaped, golden-yellow flowers, ¾in(2cm) across. Plant in autumn or spring, in full sun.

Helichrysum petiolatum LIQUORICE (LICORICE) PLANT A shrubby perennial with lax, semi-trailing stems to 2ft(60cm) or more long. Grown for its small, woolly, grey leaves, to 1½in(4cm) long, which form an excellent foil for bright-coloured summer flowers in containers and hanging baskets. Their small creamy flowers may appear in summer, but are best discouraged by hard spring pruning to maintain good leaf colour. Plant in mid-spring in full sun; in colder areas overwinter under glass or propagate

annually by cuttings taken in autumn. *H. microphyllum* is similar, but has tiny leaves and less vigorous growth.

Heliotropium × **hybridum** HELIOTROPE, CHERRY PIE Half-hardy shrubby perennials chiefly grown as bedding plants and suitable for window boxes, pots and hanging baskets. The sweetly scented violet-blue, mauve or purple flowers appear in clusters up to 6in(15cm) wide through summer until autumn. To 1-1½ft(30-45cm) tall. Plant out in early summer, when all danger of frost is past, in sun and shelter; pinch out growing points to encourage branching. In autumn, either discard the plants or move them to a heated greenhouse, as propagation stock. If a greenhouse is available, heliotropes can also be raised as 2ft(60cm) high standards, which look spectacular in urns underplanted with yellow-flowered and/or silvery-grey foliage plants.

Hibiscus Bushy shrubs to 8ft(2.5m) tall, though generally smaller when pot-grown. Widely trumpet-shaped flowers, generally to 4in(10cm) across, centred by a prominent column carrying the stamens and styles, appear in mid- to late summer (until autumn when summers are hot). Flower size can be increased by pruning hard in spring, though they are then less profuse. Propagate by semi-ripe cuttings or by seeds. Grow in full sun in medium-sized free-standing containers. *H. rosa-sinensis* is tender and must be overwintered in frost-free conditions. Leaves are glossy and evergreen, to 6in(15cm) long; flowers are 5in(12cm) or more across in shades of pink, red, orange, yellow or white. Numerous single and double varieties are available. *H. syriacus* (rose of Sharon) has flowers in a wide colour range from white to purple and violet. It may be trained against a sunny wall.

Hosta PLANTAIN LILIES Hardy perennials grown for their striking foliage, often prominently variegated. The funnel-shaped flowers, chiefly white and violet-purple, are borne in nodding clusters in late summer. Several of the smaller species are suitable for deep window boxes planted with other permanent plants and bulbs, or in tubs and urns. All thrive in partial shade, but do need plenty of watering in the growing season. Elevated positions help to keep the plants' worst enemy, slugs, at bay. Plant in autumn or spring, in potting compost enriched with water-retaining peat. *H. albo-marginata* grows 15-18in(38-45cm) high; the broad leaves, tapering to a point, have distinct white margins. *H. fortunei* 'Albopicta' forms leaf mounds 18in(45cm) high, which in the early stages are pale green heavily flushed with yellow. *H. undulata*, 2ft(60cm) high, has gently wavy, oblong leaves, green and with prominent silvery-white markings.

Humulus lupulus 'Aureus' HOP A golden-leaved form of the commercial hop. The leaves are lobed, 3-6in(8-15cm) long, and borne on herbaceous, twining stems, climbing to 10-20ft(3-6m). Male and female flowers are borne, female ones having clusters of greenish papery bracts. Plant in autumn or spring, against a sunny wall and in good loamy soil; provide trellis support.

Hyacinthus orientalis DUTCH HYACINTHS Extremely popular as forced indoor bulbs for winter flowers, they are very hardy and ideal for mid- to late spring flowering in outdoor window boxes and containers. Funnel-shaped, reflexing, waxy flowers in a wide range of shades including yellow, white and numerous shades of pink and blue are borne in very dense cylindrical heads up to 6in(15cm) long, slightly before the fleshy, strap-shaped leaves; most varieties have a beautiful sweet fragrance. To 8-12in(20-30cm) tall. Plant bulbs 6in(15cm) deep in early autumn in a sunny site ('second'- or 'bedding'-size bulbs, or those that have previously flowered indoors, are suitable for outdoors). A vast number of named hybrids are available.

Hydrangea Deciduous, hardy, woody shrubs, most of which are bushy, though a few are climbers.

Flowers appear in summer in tight, rounded clusters or sometimes of 'lace-cap' formation with sterile ray florets in a ring around less showy and very small fertile florets. Propagate by semi-ripe cuttings in summer; plant in moist, loamy soil in autumn or spring in light shade. *H. anomala petiolaris* (common or Japanese climbing hydrangea) climbs to 65-80ft(20-25m) with age, bearing finely toothed leaves and flat 7-10in(18-25cm) wide heads of whitish flowers in early summer. Self-supporting but they need some help at first. *H. macrophylla* (*H. hortensis*) is represented by numerous hybrids, the flower colour of which may vary from pink/red to mauve/blue, according to the pH of the soil (alkaline to acid respectively) and the variety, or sometimes white (on any soil). Though with maturity these plants are moderate-sized rounded shrubs, young ones are commonly grown as pot-plants and may be used in window boxes and other containers. The hortensia or mop-headed varieties with their 5-8in(12-20cm) heads are best for this purpose since they produce flowers on quite young plants.

Iberis umbellata CANDYTUFT A hardy 6-16in(15-40cm) tall annual with pink, pinkish-purple or white flowers in flattish heads to 2in(5cm) across in summer; leaves are lance-shaped. Sow seeds in succession from early spring to late spring in a sunny position where they are to flower, or sow under glass in late winter. Discard plants at the end of the season.

Ilex HOLLIES The hardy evergreen hollies, with usually spiny leaves and bright red berry clusters in winter, do not come readily to mind as subjects for window boxes and other containers. A few, however, are of diminutive size and ideally suited to the winter window box, and others make outstanding specimen shrubs planted in tubs one either side of windows and doors. Berries are produced only if a male holly is situated in the vicinity of a female. Plant in late spring, watering often until young plants are established in sun or shade, variegated forms pre-

ferably in full sun. Pruning is not normally necessary, but hollies can be trimmed to shape without any adverse effect; on variegated types cut out shoots which revert to green. The following make handsome additions to window boxes: *I. cornuta* 'Dwarf Burford' (female), about 1ft(30cm), compact and slow-growing, with glossy green leaves, spiny or entire; and 'Rotunda', equally dwarf, of rounded growth and with heavily spined leaves. *I. crenata* 'Golden Gem', up to 1½ft(45cm), is non-berrying, but attractive for its ovate leaves, golden in summer and yellowish-green in winter and spring; 'Mariesii' is even smaller, a compact miniature dome crowded with tiny rounded leaves. *I. × altaclarensis* 'Golden King' and *I. aquifolium* 'Silver Queen', female and male respectively in spite of their names, make handsome specimen shrubs for tubs where they rarely exceed 4ft(1.2m). 'Golden King', with large red berries, has broad, spineless leaves, heavily edged with golden-yellow; in 'Silver Queen' the foliage is margined with silver.

Impatiens wallerana (*I. holstii*) BUSY LIZZIE, PATIENT LUCY A tender and succulent 10-12in(15-30cm) tall perennial, popular as a house-plant but which may be treated as a half-hardy annual, planted outdoors in a cool semi-shaded spot in summer. Flowers are flat, 1-1½in(2.5-4cm) wide with a short spur, in shades of pink, scarlet, crimson, maroon, orange or white (some varieties are striped white). Leaves may be mid-green or bronze-red. Sow seed varieties under glass in early spring; plant out or into their final containers in late spring to early summer in moist compost.

Ipomoea MORNING GLORIES Half-hardy annuals of climbing and twining habit, bearing trumpet-shaped, profuse but often transient flowers from mid-summer onwards; leaves are mostly heart-shaped. Sow seeds under glass in spring (to aid germination the seed should be soaked in water overnight, or the outer covering should be chipped). Plant outdoors in early summer in a light, rich soil in a sunny site. These are ideal plants for growing around a window, trained on wires or trellis from a ground-level container or border. Deadhead. *I. alba* (*I. bona-nox, Calonyction aculeatum,* moon flower) climbs to 10ft(3m) with pure white 6in(15cm) wide flowers; *I. nil* (Japnese morning glory) reaches a similar height with violet, rose or blue 2in(5cm) wide flowers (var 'Scarlett O'Hara' has larger scarlet flowers); *I. purpurea* (*Pharbitis purpurea, Convolvulus purpureus,* common morning glory) is more vigorous with white, red or purple 5in(12cm) long flowers; *I. tricolor* (*I. rubro-coerulea, Pharbitis tricolor*) climbs to 8ft(2.5m) with reddish-purple or blue, yellow-throated, 4in(10cm) long flowers.

Jasminum JASMINES, JESSAMINES This genus includes some of the most sweetly scented shrubby climbers, especially suitable for training around a window from open ground. Their small trumpet-shaped flowers are mainly white or yellow. Propagate from semi-ripe or hardwood cuttings or by layering; plant in any soil in sun or partial shade in late autumn or spring, provide support, and tie in as necessary. *J. mesnyi* (*J. primulinum,* primrose jasmine) is moderately hardy, to 15ft(4-5m), with semi-double yellow 1½in(4cm) long flowers in spring. *J. nudiflorum* (winter-flowering jasmine) is a very hardy, semi-prostrate, 5ft(1.5m) tall green-stemmed shrub which needs tying to its support. Bright yellow flowers are borne on naked branches in mid-winter. *J. officinale* (common white jasmine) is hardy and deciduous, to 30ft(9m), but with weak stems and requiring careful support. White 1½in(4cm) long flowers are borne in summer. *J. polyanthum* is moderately hardy, usually evergreen, to 25ft(7.5m) tall, with clusters of pink-flushed white 1in(2.5cm) long flowers in late spring to summer. *J. × stephanense* is a moderately hardy semi-evergreen hybrid, to 15ft(4.5m), with clusters of pale pink, ½in(1.5cm) long flowers in early summer.

Juniperus JUNIPERS Very hardy evergreen conifers with needle- or awl-shaped juvenile leaves and scale-like, tiny adult leaves. The species are mostly upright trees, but numerous dwarf varieties are suitable for containers. Propagate by semi-ripe or hardwood heel cuttings in summer and autumn; plant in spring or autumn in full sun or partial shade. *J. chinensis* (Chinese juniper) dwarf variety: 'Pyramidalis' (pyramidal, silver-blue, to 5ft[1.5m]). *J. communis* dwarf variety: 'Compressa' (Noah's Ark juniper, perfect column, dark green, to 18in(45cm). *J. horizontalis* (creeping juniper) dwarf prostrate variety: 'Grey Pearl' (compact, grey, to 6 × 16in[15 × 40cm]). *J. × media* varieties: 'Pfitzerana Old Gold' (spreading and semi-prostrate, bronze-gold, to 2½ × 5ft[0.75 × 1.5m] and 'Blaauw' (vase-shaped, bluish grey-green, to 5ft[1.5m]). *J. squamata* dwarf variety: 'Blue Star' (rounded, silver-blue, to 16in[40cm]).

Kochia scoparia trichophylla BURNING BUSH, SUMMER CYPRESS A fast-growing half-hardy annual grown for its beautiful feathery foliage which is brilliant lime-green throughout the summer, turning to deep red or purplish in autumn. Forming a very neat globular or oval bush up to 2ft(60cm) high, this plant provides an excellent foil to flowering plants. Plant out in early summer after all frost is past, in deep window boxes or containers in a sunny position.

Laburnum GOLDEN CHAIN, GOLDEN RAIN Hardy deciduous trees and shrubs, popular for their yellow, drooping flower clusters in late spring and early summer. Easy to grow, they make handsome specimen shrubs in the open or against walls; the more vigorous species can also be trained as wall coverings. Leaves of all laburnums are trifoliate and fresh- to mid-green. Flowers are pea-like, with a faint scent; the seed pods, and the leaves, are poisonous. Plant in autumn, in any kind of soil and in sun or light shade; for wall shrubs provide staking for the first few years. Pruning is rarely necessary. *L. alpinum* is the most vigorous species, eventually growing to 20ft(6m) high; pendent flower racemes, 10in(25cm) long, cascade like a golden waterfall in early summer. *L. anagyroides* grows almost as tall, and spreads with age; yellow flowers, 6-10in(15-25cm) long, appear from late spring onwards. *L. × watereri* 'Vossii' resembles *L. alpinum,* but rarely reaches the same height; the leaves are lightly hairy, and the flower racemes are even more profuse and up to 1ft(30cm) long.

Lathyrus Mostly tall, tendrilled climbers requiring deep and rather rich soil. Their 1-1½in(2.5-3.5cm) pea-flowers are usually very sweetly fragrant and have long been firm favourites in cottage gardens and as cut flowers. Sow seeds under glass in spring (chipping and/or soaking the seed aids germination). When large enough to handle, pot up seedlings individually; plant out in late spring into a good loamy soil in full sun. Feed regularly with liquid fertilizer if grown in containers. *L. latifolius* (everlasting/perennial pea) is an ultra-hardy perennial with large rose to purple or white flowers throughout summer. It is best planted in garden soil below a window where it can scramble; provide support. *L. odoratus* (sweet pea) is an annual with numerous named varieties in a range of colours including pink, salmon, red, mauve-blue, purple, cream and white. Most are tall, but a number of dwarf non-climbing varieties, not requiring support, are ideal container plants; these are mostly mixed colour series.

Laurus nobilis SWEET BAY, BAY LAUREL A moderately hardy, dense, pyramidal-shaped evergreen shrub. It will eventually reach 12-30ft(3.5-9m), but when grown in large containers it is commonly clipped formally to maintain any shape or size. Leaves are dark green, lance-shaped and rather stiff. Propagate by semi-ripe cuttings; plant in spring in a sheltered sunny site; pinch out tip when plant has reached the desired height and prune as necessary thereafter. Varieties include *angustifolia* (willow-leaf bay, narrowly lance-shaped leaves) and 'Aurea' (golden-yellow).

Lavandula angustifolia (*L. spica, L.officinalis, L. vera*) LAVENDER A very hardy dwarf evergreen shrub with very fragrant leaves and flowers, growing 2-4ft(60-120cm) or more. Leaves are very narrow and silvery-grey to grey-green. Flowers are grey-blue to purple in slender spikes on upright stems in summer. Propagate by hardwood cuttings; plant in autumn or spring in a warm sunny position. Trim plants after flowering and cut straggly plants back hard in spring. Varieties include: 'Hidcote' (2½ft [75cm] compact, violet blue); 'Munstead' (2½ft [75cm] compact, green leaves, blue-purple flowers); and 'Vera' ([Dutch lavender] 4ft [1.2m] robust and compact, blue-purple).

Lilium LILIES Among the most stately of all bulbs, these generally very hardy plants bear fragrant and characteristic flowers on slender leafy stems. Flowers are six-lobed, trumpet-shaped or flat to reflexing and borne in loose clusters or singly. Plant most bulbs 4-6in(10-15cm) deep, but *L. candidum* just 1in(2.5cm) deep, in autumn or early spring in humus-enriched soil in large tubs or pots, or in open soil under a window, in full sun or partial shade. Tall types will need staking. *L. auratum* (gold-rayed lily) has profusely crimson-spotted white flowers to 1ft(30cm) wide, each petal with a prominent gold band, in late summer; *L. candidum* (Madonna lily) has clusters of waxy, white, horizontal trumpets to 3in(8cm) long with golden anthers in early summer. Leaves are basal, appearing in autumn and persisting through the winter. To 4-5ft(1.2-1.5m) tall. *L. hansonii* has large clusters of nodding, reflexed, thick-textured, orange-yellow flowers to 2½in(6cm) wide, spotted brown, in early summer. To 4ft(1.2m) tall. *L. henryi* has loose clusters of horizontal and reflexed, orange-yellow to apricot, 3½in(9cm) long flowers with brown spots and deep orange anthers in mid- to late summer. To 8ft(2.5m) tall. *L. longiflorum* (Easter lily) half hardy, has horizontal, trumpet-shaped white flowers with golden anthers, up to 7in(18cm) long in small heads in midsummer. 'Holland's Glory' is more har-

dy than the species. To 3ft(90cm) tall. *L. regale* (regal or royal lily) is ultrahardy with loose heads of profuse trumpet-shaped flowers to 6in(15cm) long in midsummer; flowers are white, shaded sulphur-yellow in the throat and shaded rose or purplish outside. To 4-6ft(1.2-1.8m) tall. *L. tigrinum* (now *L. lancifolium*, tiger lily) has large clusters of nodding, brilliant orange-red flowers to 5in(12cm) across, with purple-black spots and prominent orange-brown anthers, in late summer. To 4-6ft(1.2-1.8m) tall. Consult specialist catalogues for suitable varieties and hybrids.

Lobelia erinus A very popular half-hardy perennial treated as an annual. Bushy and trailing varieties are invaluable for hanging baskets and containers. Tiny blue, carmine, pinkish or white flowers, often with a white eye, bloom in profusion throughout the summer. Sow seeds thinly under glass in late winter. Seedlings are very tiny and cannot be individually transplanted – instead space out small clumps when large enough to handle. Plant in late spring in a partially shaded, sheltered position.

Lonicera HONEYSUCKLES The twining and woody honeysuckles are mostly hardy climbers bearing whorls of beautifully sweet-scented, trumpet-shaped flowers mainly in summer. Popular plants for cultivating near or around a window. Propagate by semi-ripe or hardwood cuttings late summer to autumn (rooted in a cold frame) or by layering. Plant deciduous species in late autumn and winter, evergreen species in late spring, in ordinary garden soil. Most climbing honeysuckles prefer their roots to be cool and shaded. Provide support and tie in leaders. *L. ×americana* is a vigorous hybrid with deciduous leaves and prolific white/yellow, purple-tinged flowers to 2in(5cm) long. *L. × brownii* (scarlet trumpet honeysuckle) is a deciduous or semi-evergreen hybrid with orange-scarlet flowers (scarlet-red in variety 'Dropmore Scarlet') to 1½in(4cm) long in late spring, and repeating in late summer. *L. japonica* is very vigorous with semi-evergreen or evergreen leaves and white

to yellow 1½in(4cm) fragrant flowers. The variety 'Aureoreticulata' is less vigorous but grown for its yellow-patterned leaves. *L. periclymenum* (woodbine) is the most commonly grown species, with deciduous leaves and creamy-white 2in(5cm) fragrant flowers from pinkish-mauve buds. 'Belgica' (early Dutch honeysuckle), compact and flowers in late spring; 'Serotina' (late Dutch honeysuckle), vigorous and later-flowering. *L. sempervirens* (trumpet honeysuckle), is hardy in parts of North America, but needs a warm sheltered site in northern gardens. It is evergreen or semi-evergreen with 2in(5cm) long orange-scarlet flowers. *L. tragophylla* is deciduous with large golden flowers up to 3½in(9cm) long, good in shade.

Lysimachia nummularia CREEPING JENNY An ultra-hardy, trailing, evergreen perennial with small rounded leaves and cup-shaped, ½-¾in(1-2cm) yellow flowers in summer. Good for trailing over edges of containers or hanging baskets. Stems reach 2ft(60cm). Propagate by stem cuttings in spring or autumn, rooted in their flowering position, or by division; thrives in any location, but needs moisture. 'Aurea' has bright golden leaves.

Magnolia Hardy deciduous and evergreen trees and shrubs, magnificent in bloom and well worth the special care they need. With a few exceptions magnolias do not thrive in limy soils, and their sites should be carefully chosen, with shelter from cold winds and, for spring-flowering types, away from the direct path of morning sun which, after frost, may damage the flower buds. Evergreen magnolias make spectacular wall shrubs, and a few deciduous species can be grown in deep pots and tubs. Plant in spring, staking young plants until established. *M. grandiflora* (bull bay, laurel/southern magnolia), height 15ft(4.5m) or more, is one of the finest evergreen wall shrubs, with ovate, dark green glossy leaves, rusty-brown on the undersides. Scented, bowl-shaped, creamy-white flowers, up to 8in(20cm) across, bloom throughout summer. Plant at the foot of a sheltered wall, in deep loamy soil; on mature plants prune out straggly shoots in spring. *M. stellata* (star magnolia) is deciduous and 5ft(1.5m) high and wide, of rounded habit. Slow-growing and suitable for deep pots and tubs. The pale green leaves appear simultaneously with or shortly after the starry, fragrant flowers, up to 4in(10cm) wide, in mid-spring; they are pure white in the species, pink in named varieties.

Matthiola incana STOCK A moderately hardy upright or bushy biennial, bearing dense erect heads of 1in(2.5cm) flowers in most colours except true blue and orange. Usually offered as particular strains in mixed colours with single or double flowers, but selected strains are usually cultivated. Leaves are narrow, downy and grey green. Height: 1-2½ft(30-75cm). Sow seeds under glass in early spring; plant out in mid- to late spring in sun or partial shade in a rich soil. Varieties may be classified into three main categories. Brompton varieties, grown as biennials for spring flowering, reaching 1½-2ft(45-60cm); Intermediate (East Lothian) varieties can be similarly treated or grown as winter-sown half-hardy annuals, reaching 16-18in(40-45cm). Varieties grown as annuals for summer show include Trysomic (seven week) stocks with a bushy and sturdy habit, to 1½ft(45cm), flowering within 7-8 weeks from sowing, mainly double-flowered; and Ten-week varieties flowering within 10-12 weeks from sowing, with tall, single flowers in rather dense inflorescences.

Mesembryanthemum criniflorum LIVINGSTONE DAISY · Half-hardy annual, often listed under various other botanical names but unmistakable for its myriad of brightly coloured, narrow-petalled flowers throughout summer. Rarely reaching a height of 6in(15cm), the spreading plants are ideal as edgings to window boxes and shallow pots. Leaves are narrow and pale green, often with a 'frosty' covering; daisy flowers, 1in(2.5cm) across,

are bright orange, apricot, pink and carmine, often with contrasting paler zones. Set out plants in mid- to late spring; drought and wind-resistant they demand full sun.

Mimulus MONKEY FLOWERS Correctly short-lived perennials, but usually treated as half-hardy annuals, monkey flowers are among the few doing best in shady window boxes and pots, given copious water throughout the season. Plant young seedlings in mid-spring; in autumn either discard the plants or pot them up and overwinter indoors or in a cool greenhouse. *M. cupreus*, 6in(15cm) high, is mound-forming with small, oblong, greenish-grey leaves and short-spurred flowers. The open-faced 2in(5cm) across flowers bloom all summer. They are chiefly in shades of red and orange-yellow, usually spotted with red. *M. variegatus* is somewhat taller, up to 1ft(30cm), with similar leaves and larger, more heavily blotched flowers.

Muscari GRAPE HYACINTHS Very hardy dwarf bulbs with grass-like leaves and crowded, short spikes of tiny urn-shaped or globular flowers, mostly in shades of blue or white, in mid-spring. Good for edging containers. Plant bulbs 2-3in(5-8cm) deep in early autumn in a sunny site. *M. botryoides* has white-rimmed, deep blue flowers on 6-8in(15-20cm) stems. 'Album' has white flowers. *M. armeniacum* has tapering spikes of white-rimmed cobalt blue flowers on 8-12in(20-30cm) stems. The leaves appear in autumn and overwinter. 'Blue Spike' has double flowers in large dense heads; 'Early Giant' has deep cobalt blue flowers in large heads.

Myosotis sylvatica GARDEN OR WOOD FORGET-ME-NOT A spring-flowering bushy, hardy biennial bearing profuse sprays of tiny blue, pink or white flowers, each with a white and yellow eye, opening from pinkish/mauve buds. From 6-16in(15-40cm) in height: taller varieties provide an excellent foil for spring bulbs; dwarf varieties are good for edges of containers. Sow seed in late spring in a cold frame or in open ground; transplant in autumn.

Narcissus NARCISSI AND DAFFODILS Very popular hardy, spring-flowering bulbs mostly with characteristic yellow or white, trumpet-shaped flowers, and narrow, strap-shaped leaves. Many species are in cultivation, together with hundreds of hybrids that are classified according to flower shape and parentage. Plant small bulbs 3-4in(8-10cm) deep and larger bulbs 4-6in(10-15cm) deep in early autumn, in full sun. After flowering deadhead but do not disturb bulbs until leaves have died down naturally. Bulbs may be lifted during summer if containers need to be re-planted. Available species and hybrids are too numerous to list in detail: consult specialist catalogues.

Nemesia strumosa MOSAIC OF JEWELS A colourful, 8-18in(20-45cm) tall, half-hardy annual with clusters of profuse, funnel-shaped, 1in(2.5cm) flowers in bright or pastel shades of yellow, orange, red, purple, blue or white, often with a contrasting eye, borne in early to midsummer; leaves are narrow and toothed. Sow seeds in early spring under glass; plant outdoors in late spring after all danger of frost is past, in window boxes and containers in full sun. Shear off dead flowers to encourage a second growth.

Nepeta CATMINT, CATNIP Hardy perennials, easy to grow in sun or shade and ideal for container culture, being undemanding and remaining in bloom from late spring until well into autumn. Plant in autumn or spring and cut back to crown level when flowering has finished. *N. × faasseni*, height 12-15in(30-38cm), is suitable for window boxes and other containers; from late spring the narrow, grey-green foliage is almost obscured by the flower stems set with whorls of small, lavender-blue flowers. *N. hederacea* 'Variegata', only 4in(10cm) high, is also ideal for hanging baskets, trailing its stems as much as 1½ft(45cm); leaves are toothed and kidney-shaped, pale green marked with white; the flowers are deep blue.

Nerine bowdenii A moderately hardy 2ft(60cm) tall bulb suitable for large containers or for planting beneath a window. Pale pink flowers to 3in(8cm) wide, with narrow, wavy and frilled petals and prominent stamens, are borne in large, elegant inflorescences in late summer to autumn. Strap-shaped leaves appear after the flowers, dying down the following summer. Plant bulbs 4-6in(10-15cm) deep in early summer in a warm, sunny, sheltered position or in containers (4in[10cm] pots for 1 bulb and 5-6in[12.5-15cm] for 3 or 4 bulbs). Keep containers in a frost-free place over winter. Repot every 4 years or so. Varieties include 'Fenwick's Variety' (deep pink), 'Pink Beauty' (deep pink) and 'Pink Triumph' (silvery-pink).

Nerium oleander OLEANDER A tender, bushy and suckering evergreen shrub widely grown outdoors in Mediterranean regions. Elsewhere it may be grown outdoors in summer in large pots or tubs which should be kept moist in summer. Fragrant 1-2in(2.5-5cm) flowers appear in clusters in spring and summer, in shades or red, pink, salmon or white (double-flowered varieties also). Leaves are lance-shaped, often in threes, up to 10in(25cm) long; variegated with cream in the variety 'Variegatum'. It grows up to 10ft(3m) or less if pruned. Propagate by semi-ripe cuttings; plant in containers, or in open ground against a wall in full sun. Leaves are very toxic.

Nicotiana alata (*N. affinis*) FLOWERING TOBACCO An erect and sticky-haired, half-hardy annual with long-tubed starry yellow, white, pink through scarlet to deep mauve, or lime-green flowers, each 1-2in(2.5-5cm) across, in loose clusters throughout the summer. Many have a glorious heavy fragrance when the flowers open in the evening. Sow seeds under glass in early spring; plant outdoors in late spring after all danger of frost is past. Tobacco plants grow best in rich soil in full sun, though if planted in shade the flowers open all day rather than just in the evening. Feed occasionally with liquid fertilizer. Dwarf varieties and hybrids, listed under *N.* × *sanderae*, are most

suitable for containers, reaching 1-2ft(30-60cm) in height: in contrast to tall varieties, these bear flowers which open in the daytime.

Oenothera missouriensis OZARK SUNDROPS A hardy 6-12in(15-30cm) tall, low-growing perennial, with lance-shaped, bright green leaves; suitable for the permanent window box or container. The lemon-yellow flowers, sometimes with a faint scent, are unusual in opening from narrow, red-spotted funnels into wide-open, 4in(10cm) blooms in the evening throughout summer. Plant in autumn or spring, in full sun; in autumn cut stems and withered foliage back to crown level.

Olearia × **haastii** DAISY BUSH Hardy evergreen, summer-flowering shrub. In the open garden it forms a rounded bush, about 6ft(1.8m) high, but grown in a deep pot or tub the average size is considerably less. Thriving in city conditions, it is spectacular sited in full sun near windows through which can drift the fragrance of the white daisy flowers which give the plant its name. They bloom throughout summer in 3in(8cm) wide clusters which almost smother the ovate, glossy leaves, felted white on the undersides. Plant in spring or autumn, in good potting compost; pruning generally unnecessary, cut out any spindly or frost-damaged shoots in spring.

Paeonia PEONIES These hardy and long-lived herbaceous perennials are chiefly grown in the open garden where they can avoid the root disturbance they dislike so much. Most peonies are named varieties from the species *P. lactiflora*; they can be grown in tubs of good compost thoroughly mixed with well-rotted manure so that the fleshy roots will not exhaust the soil too quickly. The flowers, up to 8in(20cm) across, are bowl-shaped, single, semi- or fully-double, fragrant in some hybrids, and span a colour range from pure glistening white through shades of pink and red; many have prominent golden stamens. Specialist catalogues should be consulted for choice. Set the crowns fairly shallowly (1in[2.5cm]

deep) in early autumn and site containers in good light, shaded from morning sun and protected from strong winds. The early summer-flowering season is short but spectacular; deadhead as necessary and cut the foliage back close to the crowns in autumn.

Parthenocissus VIRGINIA CREEPERS, WOODBINE Self-supporting, vigorous, hardy, deciduous climbers valued for their rich autumn colours. Most species can easily cover a two- or even three-storey building; their suckered tendrils are very difficult to clear from paintwork, etc., when decoration is carried out, but if this does not worry the occupier, they make excellent wall coverings, often encroaching on window frames dramatically. Propagate by cuttings or by layering; plant in neutral or alkaline soil in open ground. *P. henryana* (Chinese Virginia creeper) has leaves of three or five white-veined leaflets turning red in autumn. *P. himalayana* (Himalayan Virginia creeper) has leaves of three leaflets turning to deep crimson in autumn. *P. quinquefolia* (true Virginia creeper) is extremely vigorous with leaves comprising five leaflets and brilliant warm-red autumn colours. *P. tricuspidata* (Boston ivy) has variable leaves, mainly three-lobed, and with rather harsh crimson autumn colours.

Passiflora PASSION FLOWERS Tendrilled woody climbers to 15ft(4.5m) with unusual, short-lived, starry flowers in summer, sometimes followed by yellow or orange, egg-like, edible fruits. Leaves are generally lobed. Most species are rather tender and may be cut down by frosts, but in milder or sheltered sites these are interesting plants for training around a window from open ground. Propagate by semi-ripe cuttings in summer; plant in late spring in a well-drained soil and provide adequate support. Water freely in summer. *P. caerulea* (blue passion flower) has 3-4in(7.5-10cm) wide white flowers with a blue/purple, fringe-like corona (pure white in 'Constance Elliott') and flowers well in pots. Nearly fully hardy, surviving mild frosts but best protected. *P. edulis* (purple granadilla, passion fruit) is similar to *P. caerulea* but with slightly smaller flowers. It bears delicious purple to greenish-brown fruits in warm climates. Not hardy.

Pelargonium Evergreen sub-shrubs, commonly referred to as geraniums, though botanically distinct, with rather succulent stems, becoming woody with age. They bear five-petalled flowers, or frequently semi-doubles or doubles, in rounded clusters; a vast range of colours including pink, red, orange, mauve and white. Leaves are variable in shape, forming a part-basis for the classification of this genus. All are very popular for container planting. Propagate by cuttings taken in late summer; overwinter under protection from frosts. If only small plants are required, cuttings may be taken in early spring from overwintered plants; or propagate by seed sown over heat under glass in late winter (F_1 hybrids are now commonly grown as half-hardy annuals from seed). Plant or place containers in full sun or partial shade outdoors in early summer. Pelargoniums need regular watering and feeding during the summer but should be kept on the dry side; overwinter in cool temperatures. Deadhead. Regal pelargoniums have lobed, toothed and often rather fluted leaves and umbels of large, often frilly flowers, each to 2in(5cm) across. Zonal pelargoniums have rounded leaves with scalloped margins and characteristically with a central ring of bronzy colouring (some with variegated colouring). Flowers appear in tight heads, to 6in(15cm) wide. Many modern strains, easily raised from seed, and being dwarf and brightly flowered, are excellent for window boxes. Ivy-leaved pelargoniums have trailing stems reaching up to 3ft(90cm) in length, making them ideal trailing subjects for hanging baskets and window boxes. Their flowers are in small umbels. Scented-leaved pelargoniums are grown chiefly for their lemon-, nutmeg-, mint-scented, etc., leaves, which are very fragrant when bruised.

Pernettya mucronata Hardy evergreen shrub, chiefly grown for its large clusters of bright berries in autumn and winter. Excellent as additions to window boxes where height is usually confined to 12-18in(30-45cm). Tiny, bell-shaped dainty white flowers appear in profuse clusters in early summer and followed by white, pink, red or purple berries which persist for months. Wiry stems form dense clumps of small, glossy dark green, sharp-pointed leaves. The plants are unisexual, and a male must be planted among the females to ensure berry production. They are also lime-haters and therefore need an acid potting compost; tolerant of shade, they bloom and fruit best in full sun. Plant in early autumn or late spring; pruning generally unnecessary.

Petunia × hybrida Very popular half-hardy 8-16in(20-40cm) tall annuals for containers, with profuse and extremely showy funnel-shaped flowers in a range of colours including red, purple, blue, pink, salmon, yellow and white, also bicolours, throughout summer. Leaves are pale green and sticky. Sow seeds under glass in early spring; plant out in late spring to early summer into a light soil in a sheltered, sunny position. There are numerous named varieties classified according to flower size and type (these include some double-flowered varieties). Multiflora varieties have profuse, medium-sized 2-3in(5-8cm) wide flowers on bushy plants. Grandiflora varieties have fewer, larger flowers, up to 5in(12cm) wide, and are often frilled. Pendula varieties of trailing habit are particularly useful for window boxes and hanging baskets. Nana Compacts varieties are dwarf, reaching just 6in(15cm). F_1 hybrids, when available, are to be recommended because they have larger flowers and the plants are more uniform and sturdier.

Phormium tenax NEW ZEALAND FLAX An evergreen perennial grown for its exotic foliage. Half-hardy in most temperate climates it often succeeds better as a container plant which can be moved under frost-free cover in winter. It forms a fan, about 6ft(1.8m) high, of narrow, strap-shaped and leathery leaves, mid- or dark green in the species, deep purple in the variety 'Purpureum'. Tall stems bear branched heads of rather dull, reddish flowers on established plants in summer. Dwarf varieties and hybrids with variegated leaves are also available. Plant in late spring in large terracotta pots and place in a sunny and sheltered site; in cold areas protect the crowns with straw or move pots under cover.

Plumbago capensis (*P. auriculata*) CAPE PLUMBAGO A semi-hardy, semi evergreen lax climber often grown under glass, but suitable for growing in containers or hanging baskets outdoors in milder climates and flowering well in pots when young. Clusters of pale blue (white in 'Alba') primrose-shaped flowers, each 1in(2.5cm) wide, bloom throughout summer, and in frost-free areas flowers may be produced all year. If supported, Cape plumbago grows to 12ft(3.5m). Propagate by semi-ripe heel cuttings in summer; plant outdoors in early summer and water freely; overwinter under protection, keeping plants just moist.

Polygonum baldschuanicum RUSSIAN VINE, MILE-A-MINUTE Few climbers can rival the Russian vine for vigour and tenacity. Capable of extending growth by 10ft(3m) or more in a single season, this hardy deciduous twiner is excellent for covering unsightly walls and fences. The bright green leaves are obscured in the summer months by billowing creamy-white flower sprays, as much as 1½ft(45cm) long. Plant in autumn or spring. Easily grown in any type of soil, in sun or shade, the only attention it needs is support of strong wires round which it can twine, and ruthless pruning in spring to contain it within the allotted wall space.

Primula POLYANTHUS AND PRIMROSES A group of showy, clump-forming plants with flowers in a very wide range of colours, including strong and pastel shades, generally with a yellow eye and including bicolours and tricolours. Polyanthus (*P. × tommasinii, P. vulgaris elatior, P. veris elatior, P. × polyantha*) have bright 1½-2in(4-5cm) flowers in rounded clusters – on single stems from late winter to spring. To 8in(20cm) in height. Florists' primroses (*P. vulgaris* hybrids) are similar, but their flowers appear singly on each stem, rather than in clusters, in spring and early summer. Sow seeds of polyanthus and primroses in summer in a cold frame, covering with glass to maintain humidity; plant into flowering position in autumn, choosing a partially shaded site. Water plants freely. Seed is usually sold as mixed colour series.

Prunus ORNAMENTAL CHERRIES Hardy and mainly deciduous trees and shrubs, popular for garden and street planting and beloved for their brief but magnificent flower display. They are popular trained as Bonsai subjects, and a few are suitable for growing in deep pots and tubs where the confinement of the root system keeps a check on height and usually results in more prolific flowers. Plant in autumn, in good potting compost top-dressed annually and fed during the growing season; sun or light shade. Any necessary pruning should be done in late summer to avoid 'bleeding'. *P. incisa* (Fuji cherry), of shrubby habit, can be kept to a height of 5ft(1.5m); leaves are mid-green, sharply toothed and with brilliant autumn colours. Small flowers, ¾in(2cm) wide, open white from pink buds along the naked branches in early spring. *P. subhirtella* 'Autumnalis' also bears white, but semi-double flowers, during autumn and winter; frequent pinching out of the shoots keeps it manageable as a container plant and encourages flowering; the weeping form 'Pendula', with pink flowers, is especially attractive.

Pyracantha FIRETHORNS Spiny evergreen woody shrubs with narrow toothed leaves to 2-3in(5-8cm) long. Profuse clusters of tiny, creamy-white flowers in early summer are followed by persistent red, orange or yellow berries in autumn. Most are very hardy, and may be trained as espaliers against a wall and around a window, grown in open ground. Height: 8-23ft(2.5-7m) according to species. Propagate by

semi-ripe heel cuttings in late summer or by layering; plant between autumn and spring in fine weather, in fertile soil in full sun or partial shade. Provide support such as wires or trellis, tying in leaders securely (mature plants may be rather heavy). Prune unwanted growth in early summer. *P. atalantioides* is very vigorous with dark glossy leaves. Fruits are scarlet, or yellow in 'Aurea'. *P. coccinea* is similar to above but not so tall growing and with profuse dense bunches of dark red fruits. Hybrids of various species have given rise to some fine orange-red/yellow fruiting varieties.

Reseda odorata MIGNONETTE A hardy annual with erect heads of greenish-yellow flowers, each with a tuft of rust-orange stamens; showier varieties with reddish or golden flowers are often available. Though not very showy, these plants have a rich, sweet perfume making them wonderful subjects for a window box or growing below a window. Height to 1½ft(45cm). Sow seeds under glass in early spring; plant out in late spring into a quite rich, alkaline soil in full sun. Where possible, seeds should be direct-sown into their flowering position in mid-spring, because mignonettes do not like being transplanted. Space out seedlings about 6in(15cm) apart.

Rhododendron JAPANESE AZALEAS Semi-evergreen ericaceous shrubs bearing profuse clusters of funnel-shaped or flattish 1½-2½in(4-6cm) flowers in mid- to late spring. Leaves are small, ¾-1½in(2-4cm) long and often acquire rich autumn tints. Most Japanese azaleas reach 3-6ft(1-1.8m) when mature, though young plants often bear equally profuse flowers and are ideal container plants. All are generally frost-hardy. Propagate by semi-ripe cuttings; plant in autumn in acid soil in a cool shady position (azaleas hate lime, dry roots and direct sun). Provide a base fertilizer each spring; ideally, grow azaleas in their own container, where their particular soil requirements can be met. Species and hybrids with flowers ranging from white through

yellow to pink and mauve are widely available.

Rosa ROSES Very familiar and much-loved, deciduous, generally thorny shrubs with beautiful fragrant flowers. Of the many classified types only the climbers and miniatures are really suited for window gardens, the former reaching up to 20-30ft(6-9m), given adequate support, and suitable for planting at the foot of a building; the latter forming a compact dwarf bush suitable for planting in a window box or other container. Roses need good compost/soil, and though most prefer a sunny site, several climbers do well on north-facing walls. Miniatures need little pruning, but laterals of climbers should be pruned to two or three buds from the main stem in autumn or winter, and securely tied in. Climbing roses have a permanent framework of stems with lateral flowering shoots bearing large, 3-4in(8-10cm) wide flowers in late spring or early summer, sometimes until autumn; popular hybrids are too numerous to list here: consult specialist catalogues.

Rosmarinus officinalis ROSEMARY Near-hardy evergreen sub-shrub, grown for ornamental as well as culinary purposes and suitable for cultivation in window boxes and small pots where height and spread can be kept to the desired proportions by judicious pruning. The erect or lax stems are closely covered with narrowly linear, dark green leaves, striped white on the undersides and highly aromatic. Tubular flowers, ¾in(2cm) wide, appear in the leaf axils from late spring onwards. Plant in spring, in a sunny and sheltered position; snip off young sprigs for kitchen use as required and cut sprawling shoots back hard in spring.

Salpiglossis sinuata PAINTED TONGUE, VELVET FLOWER A half-hardy 1½-2 ft(45-60cm) tall annual, that flowers from midsummer until autumn in an extensive colour range of gold, rose and scarlet, mahogany-brown and blue, often with contrasting veins. Narrow, wavy-edged and pale green leaves are set along branching stems carrying a profusion of 2in(5cm) wide, funnel-shaped and velvety flowers. Set out seedlings when all danger of frost is past, in pots in full sun near windows on sheltered walls. Deadhead as necessary and discard at the end of the season; may be perennial in warm climates.

Salvia Half-hardy and hardy annuals and perennials, well known for their vivid red flower spikes in summer bedding schemes and window boxes. Most are derived from *S. splendens* (scarlet sage), a half-hardy perennial grown as an annual in temperate regions; average height 15in(38cm), though dwarf strains, 6-10in(15-25cm) tall, are available and especially suited for window boxes. Leaves are ovate, pointed and toothed, bright or dark green; the flower spikes, are made up of tightly packed tubular flowers, each about 1in(2.5cm) across. They are surrounded by bracts in the same colour as the flowers proper, appearing from mid-summer until well into autumn. Most are in shades of bright scarlet. *S. patens* (gentian sage), also a half-hardy perennial and flowering in its first season, is altogether 'quieter'. Height 15in(38cm), similar in foliage and growth habit to *S. splendens*, but the flower spikes are made up of tightly seedlings of all salvias when danger of frost is past, in a sunny site; pinch out the growing points to encourage branching, and discard when autumn frosts blacken the foliage.

Saxifraga A large family of mainly hardy evergreen perennials, low-growing and spreading to form wide mats. Natural rock plants, several are suitable for container growing. The majority are spring- and early summer-flowering, but the leaf mats retain their interest throughout the year. Plant in autumn in compost with added chalky grit or sand for drainage, and preferably in light shade. Remove faded flower stems. Mossy saxifrages, from the *dactyloides* group, do well in shady window boxes. Characterized by the mossy appearance of the 3in(8cm) high leaf hummocks of deeply cut leaves, which

vary from emerald-green to golden-yellow; in spring the clumps are studded with ½in(1cm) saucer-shaped flowers in white, yellow, pink or red. *S. umbrosa* (*S. × urbium*, London pride) thrives in containers in deep shade; graceful sprays of starry, white, pink or rosy flowers rise above fleshy, dark green leaf rosettes in late spring. The Kabschia saxifrages can be grown in shallow pans and window boxes. They form near-prostrate leaf rosettes covered with grey or silvery encrustations. In early spring, saucer-shaped flowers, up to 1in(2.5cm), rise above the foliage cushions, pure white in *S. burserana*, pale yellow in *S. b.* 'Sulphurea', and pink in *S. × 'Cranbourne'*.

Schizanthus pinnatus BUTTERFLY FLOWER, POOR MAN'S ORCHID A bushy, half-hardy annual with very profuse orchid-like 1½in(4cm) flowers in shades of pink, purple, red and white or bicoloured, all blotched with golden-yellow in the throat. Leaves are sticky and deeply incut. Usually 3-4ft(90-120cm) tall, dwarf varieties of 12-16in(30-40cm), more suitable for window boxes and small containers, are available. Sow seeds under glass in early spring and plant out in late spring for flowering in late summer in areas where summers are not too hot. In hotter climates, sow seeds under glass in autumn and overwinter under protection for late spring display outdoors. Butterfly flowers are best grown in light soil in a sheltered, sunny position. Pinch out tips early to encourage bushiness.

Scilla SQUILLS Dwarf, ultra-hardy bulbs with clusters of starry blue or white flowers on slender stems from early spring. They multiply freely and are suitable for edges of containers. Plant 2-3in(5-7.5cm) deep in early autumn in a sunny or partially shaded site. *S. bifolia* is 6-8in(15-20cm) tall, usually with just two narrow leaves per bulb and loose racemes of nodding gentian-blue ½in(1cm) flowers. 'Alba' has white flowers; 'Rosea' has shell-pink flowers. *S. sibirica* (Siberian squill) grows 4-8in(10-20cm) tall with loose racemes of nodding violet-blue bell

flowers. Varieties include 'Alba' (white), 'Spring Beauty' (larger flowers, deep blue; very early) and 'Taurica' (pale blue with dark veins; very early). *S. tubergeniana* is 3-4in(8-10cm) tall with pale blue, dark striped, 1½in(4cm) flowers which appear before the leaves.

Sedum Hardy evergreen succulents, equally attractive in leaf and flower and suitable for container cultivation. All have starry flowers, in flat-topped, rounded clusters. Plant in autumn or spring, in full sun. Several dwarf species go well in simulated window box rock gardens or as ground cover in larger containers. *S. acre* (stonecrop), 2in (5cm) high, forms mats of rounded yellow-green and overlapping leaves above which rise yellow, 1½in(4cm) wide flower heads in midsummer. *S. dasyphyllum* is even smaller, the carpeting mats composed of tiny, fleshy, blue-green leaves; the small flower heads are pure white. *S. spectabile* (ice plant, butterfly plant), a familiar garden perennial, grows 12-15in(30-38cm) high, of neat and compact habit with broadly rounded, light green leaves covered with a white farina; flower clusters, up to 6in(15cm) wide, appear in early autumn, in shades of pink and red.

Sempervivum HOUSELEEKS Hardy, low-growing evergreens, forming neat and compact rosettes of succulent leaves often brilliantly coloured. Shallow-rooting and easy of cultivation, several species are ideal for window boxes and pans, providing colour throughout the year and, in spring, good companions for small bulbs like snowdrops, aconites and crocus. Plant in autumn or spring, in full sun; the rosettes form small offshoots which are easily detached and rooted. *S. arachnoideum*, the most commonly grown species, is 1-2in(2.5-5cm) high, with dense rosettes of small, ovate and fleshy leaves, green and red-tinted, woven together with a cobweb of silvery-white hairs; star-shaped, ¾in(2cm) wide flowers, bright pinkish-red, rise above the clumps in midsummer. *S. tectorum*, slightly taller, is outstanding for its foliage; the glossy leaves, ovate and pointed, are borne in loose rosettes to display heavy suffusions of purple-maroon; the deep pink or rosy, 1in(2.5cm) or more wide flowers bloom in midsummer.

Senecio cineraria (*S. bicolor cineraria, Cineraria maritima*) SILVER-LEAVED CINERARIA, DUSTY MILLER A semi-hardy sub-shrubby perennial which is usually treated as a half-hardy annual, reaching 8-12in(20-30cm) with deeply lobed or dissected silver, woolly leaves and yellow flowers in summer. Sow seed under glass in early spring and plant out hardened-off plants in late spring in a sunny site.

Skimmia japonica A compact and low-growing, 3-5ft(1-1.5m), evergreen shrub with glossy, leathery leaves to 4in(10cm) long but slow-growing and often only reaching 1ft(30cm) after several years. Fragrant, starry, white flowers in tight clusters, opening from pink-flushed buds, appear in spring (best on male plants). These are followed by small, bright-red fruits on female plants which often persist until the following spring, when new flowers are opening. If fruits are desired, male and female plants should be grown together (the related and similar *S. reevesiana* has bisexual flowers). Propagate by semi-ripe heel cuttings in summer; plant in autumn or spring in sun or partial shade.

Solanum Mostly rather tender shrubby perennials with potato-like starry flowers in clusters in mid- or late summer. The winter or Jerusalem cherry, *S. pseudocapsicum* (*S. capsicastrum* is similar), is evergreen, 12-18in(30-45cm) tall and may, in mild or sheltered climates, be grown in containers outdoors. Its rather insignificant white flowers are followed by globular fruits, ½-¾in(1.2-2cm) across, which ripen in early winter to glossy bright scarlet. Sow seeds under glass in spring; plant outdoors in early summer. The following species, collectively known as potato vines, are woody climbers suitable for growing against a warm wall in mild climates. Propagate by half-ripe

cuttings or layers; plant in spring in well-drained open ground, provide support and tie in as necessary. *S. crispum* (Chilean potato tree) climbs to 15-20ft(4.5-6m) with lilac-blue 1in(2.5cm) flowers. *S. jasminoides* (jasmine nightshade) is a twining species reaching 10-15ft(3-4.5m) with blue, ¾-1in (2-2.5cm) flowers and yellow stamens (white in 'Album').

Stachys lanata LAMB'S TONGUE/EAR'S, WOOLLY BETONY Correctly listed botanically as *S. olympica*, this foliage plant is invaluable in bedding schemes. Hardy except in very wet or cold seasons, it is a short-lived perennial, about 1ft(30cm) high, with 4-6in(10-15cm) long, tongue-shaped leaves, soft green and heavily covered with silvery-white and velvety hairs. The small purple flower spikes in summer are insignificant. Plant in spring, or in autumn in mild areas, in sun or very light shade.

Tagetes MARIGOLDS Easily grown and popular half-hardy annuals with long-lasting, vivid mahogany-red to pale yellow flowers throughout summer and autumn; leaves are dark green and deeply divided, generally emitting a pungent scent when bruised. Sow seeds under glass in spring for planting out in early summer in a sunny site. These plants are rarely troubled by any pests or diseases. *T. erecta* varieties (African, American or Aztec marigold) reach 2-3ft(60-90cm) with a branching habit and 3-8in(8-20cm), fully double, orange to lemon-yellow flowers. *T. patula* varieties (French marigold) are compact and bushy, reaching 8-12in(20-30cm) with single, semi-double or double, 1½-2in(4-5cm) wide flowers. Many named varieties are available including bicoloured types. *T. tenuifolia* (signet or striped marigold) is usually represented by Pumila types, of a neat and bushy habit, reaching 6-10in(15-25cm) and covered with tiny, yellow to orange or bicolour, single starry flowers.

Thunbergia Twining climbers with broad-mouthed, trumpet flowers borne throughout summer. Outdoors

they can only be considered tender to semi-hardy and are often treated as half-hardy annuals. Plant in any well-drained soil, in full sun, or in pots. *T. alata* (black-eyed Susan) climbs to 10ft(3m) in a warm summer and bears orange, dark brown-eyed 1½in(4cm) flowers. This is a good plant for baskets and other containers. Sow seeds under glass in early spring and plant out in early summer. Varieties include orange, yellow or white-flowered forms. *T. grandiflora* (blue trumpet vine, clock vine) is a more vigorous climber reaching up to 20ft(6m), which may be fully perennial in milder climates. Flowers are purplish-blue, to 3in(8cm) across, in spring and summer; leaves are evergreen. Plant this species in a good, well-drained soil at the base of a wall, and provide support.

Tropaeolum NASTURTIUMS Mostly trailing or climbing plants with brightly coloured spurred and trumpet-shaped flowers, in shades of red, orange or yellow throughout summer and autumn. Avoid over rich compost/soil which promotes leaf growth at the expense of flowers); full sun. Annuals are ideal for containers; perennials should be grown in open ground and trained against a wall. *T. majus* (garden nasturtium, Indian cress) is a hardy annual of scrambling or climbing habit. Vivid, funnel-shaped flowers are borne in succession (best on poorish, dry soils); leaves, sometimes marbled, are long-stalked and round. Tall varieties climb to 6-8ft(1.8-2.5m) or trail; dwarf varieties grow to 8-18in(20-45cm). Sow seeds in early spring under glass and plant out in late spring. *T. peregrinum* (*T. canariense*, Canary creeper) is a climbing annual reaching 12ft(3.5m) or more, with blue-green, five-lobed leaves and bright yellow, fringed, 1in(2.5cm) flowers; cultivate as for *T. majus*. *T. polyphyllum* is a moderately hardy herbaceous perennial reaching 6ft(1.8m) if trained, otherwise prostrate. It bears yellow to orange, 1in(2.5cm) wide flowers with glaucous incut leaves. Tuberous roots may be lifted and overwintered under protection. *T. speciosum* (flame creeper) is a moderately hardy perennial creeper up to 10-15ft(3-4.5m) with scarlet, 1½in(4cm) wide flowers. It does best in a cool and moist climate.

Tulipa TULIPS Very popular, hardy, spring-flowering bulbs bearing vividly coloured cup- or goblet-shaped flowers, sometimes opening starry, in a very wide range of shades including bicolours. The tall, large-flowered hybrids usually bear solitary flowers on sturdy erect stems, while shorter species often bear multiple or clustered flowers. Plant smaller bulbs 3-4in(7.5-10cm) deep; larger bulbs 5-6in(12-15cm) deep, in autumn or early winter in a sunny position. Deadhead after flowering; after the leaves have died down fully lift bulbs for dry storage until the autumn. Hybrids are numerous: consult specialist catalogues.

Verbena Showy and very colourful, sun-loving plants which are often rather short-lived and best grown as half-hardy annuals. Flowers are small, white, rose-pink, crimson or purple, sometimes with white 'eyes', and borne in dense globular heads in summer and autumn. Sow seeds under glass in early spring; plant out in late spring into a rich soil in full sun. Many can also be propagated from cuttings or by root division. *V. × hybrida* (*V. × hortensis*) is bushy and semi-prostrate with 3in(8cm) flower heads on 10-12in(25-30cm) stems throughout the summer and early autumn. *V. peruviana* (*V. chamaedrifolia*) is prostrate with short stems of starry scarlet to crimson flowers. *V. tenera* 'Maonettii' ('Mahonettii') is a creeping type with white-edged rose-lilac flowers on 6in(15cm) stems.

Viburnum Generally hardy, deciduous and evergreen shrubs, attractive for their foliage, flowers and fruit. Most are easy to grow in deep pots and tubs. Plant deciduous viburnums in autumn or early spring, evergreens in mid-spring; all do best in full sun; winter-flowering types best sheltered against west-facing walls. In open ground, any soil is suitable provided it is deep and moisture-retentive; in pots and tubs use a good potting compost and top-dress annually in spring. If necessary, trim to shape, winter-flowering viburnums in mid-spring, others after flowering. *V. × burkwoodii*, up to 5ft(1.5m) as a container plant, 8ft(2.4m) as a wall shrub, is evergreen, with ovate, dark green leaves; pink-budded, tubular flowers open to flat, 3½in(9cm) wide heads, waxy and pure white in colour, sweetly fragrant, at any time during spring. *V. carlesii* flowers at the same time, with similar white and scented flowers in more rounded heads; it is deciduous, with lightly hairy, broadly ovate and dull green leaves, and a good tub plant where height rarely exceeds 4ft(1.2m). *V. tinus* (laurustinus) is a winter and spring-flowering species, best as a wall shrub. Evergreen, of slow and bushy habit, it eventually reaches 10ft(3cm) in height, with ovately lance-shaped, dark green leaves; flat flower heads, up to 4in(10cm) across, are white, pink in the bud.

Vinca minor LESSER PERIWINKLE; TRAILING OR RUNNING MYRTLE A very hardy, prostrate perennial trailing to 3ft(90cm) but covering large areas as it roots where it touches the ground, and commonly grown as a ground-cover plant under trees and shrubs, but also suitable for containers in semi- or full shade. Leaves are glossy and evergreen, to 2in(5cm) long; flowers are five-petalled, blue-mauve, to 1¼in(3.5cm) wide in late spring to midsummer. Propagate by division or by stem cuttings in autumn or spring; plant in autumn or spring in any soil. Varieties include white, deep blue and wine-red forms.

Viola × wittrockiana (*V. tricolor hortensis*) GARDEN PANSY A group of hybrids commonly treated as seed-sown hardy biennials or half-hardy annuals. They are sturdy plants forming compact clumps 6-10in(15-25cm) high with good-sized 2-4in(5-10cm) wide, flat flowers in a wide range of bright colours including blue, purple, red, orange, yellow and cream, many with bold 'faces': mixed colours and single colours are available. Sow seeds of summer-flowering varieties under glass in early spring; plant out in late spring in sun or partial shade for colour throughout summer. Sow seeds of winter-flowering varieties in a cold frame in midsummer; plant in window boxes or other containers in autumn for flowering from late autumn to spring. Deadhead for a continuous display.

Vitis GRAPE VINES Vigorous deciduous climbers grown for the brilliant crimson and scarlet autumn colouring of their large, often lobed or maple-like leaves; and also for their grape fruits. Fruits ripen and leaves colour best where summers are hot. Propagate by cuttings; plant in fine weather between autumn and spring in neutral or alkaline soil in any aspect, though best against a south- or west-facing wall. Provide adequate support and tie in young growths. *V. coignetiae* (crimson glory vine) has spectacular rounded/lobed leaves to 1ft(30cm) across and black, sour fruits; to 80ft(25m) tall. *V. vinifera* (wine grape) is the grape of commerce, but decorative varieties are available, including 'Brandt', with deeply lobed leaves and sweet, black fruits; height to 50ft(15m), usually less.

Wisteria A most beautiful, tall-growing, twining, deciduous climber with gracefully drooping racemes of pea flowers generally of bluish-mauve colour (some whites) borne in late spring. Most species are very hardy and climb up to 30ft(9m) or even more. Plant in a rich, deep, loamy soil at the foot of a building, between late autumn and spring during fine weather; provide strong support, preferably wires, and tie in leaders (with age, plants will become self-clinging by tendrils). In late winter prune all side-shoots, and in summer shorten leafy growths. *W. floribunda* (Japanese wisteria) has violet-blue flowers in hanging clusters to 10in(25cm) long, borne as the young pinnate leaves develop. 'Macrobotrys' is an excellent variety with violet-purple flowers in racemes to 3ft(90cm) long. *W. sinensis* (Chinese wisteria) is extremely vigorous with mauve or lilac flowers which open on naked branches, racemes 8-12in(20-30cm) long.

	SEASON				POSITION			HABIT				HEIGHT				FLOWER COLOUR					OTHER FEATURES		
	Spring	Summer	Autumn	Winter	Sun	Shade	Any	Upright	Bushy	Climbing	Trailing/Spreading	Under 9in(22cm)	9-18in(22-45cm)	18in-3ft(45-90cm)	Over 3ft(90cm)	White/Cream	Yellow/Orange	Pink/Red	Blue/Purple	Multicoloured	Berries/Fruits	Attractive Foliage	Scent
Actinidia kolomikta		■			■					■					■	■						■	
Agapanthus species		■	■		■			■						■		■			■				
Ageratum houstonianum		■					■		■			■							■				
Alyssum maritimum		■			■						■	■				■							■
Antirrhinum majus		■			■			■					■			■	■	■		■			
Arabis caucasica	■				■						■	■				■		■					
Armeria species	■	■			■				■			■				■		■					
Artemisia species		■			■				■					■			■					■	
Aubrieta deltoidea	■				■						■	■						■	■				
Aucuba japonica				■			■		■						■						■	■	
Begonia species		■	■		■	■			■			■	■			■	■	■		■		■	
Bellis perennis	■	■			■				■			■				■		■					
Berberis species	■	■					■		■						■		■				■	■	
Buxus species	■	■					■		■						■							■	
Calceolaria species		■			■	■			■			■	■				■	■		■			
Callistephus chinensis		■	■		■			■					■	■		■		■	■				
Camellia species	■			■		■			■						■	■		■				■	
Campanula species		■			■	■			■		■	■	■			■		■	■				
Campsis radicans		■	■		■					■					■		■	■					
Canna × generalis		■	■		■			■						■	■		■	■				■	
Ceanothus species	■	■			■				■						■	■			■				
Centaurea species		■			■			■					■	■		■		■	■				
Chaenomeles species	■			■			■		■						■	■		■			■		
Chamaecyparis species	■	■			■			■				■		■	■							■	
Cheiranthus species	■				■				■				■			■	■	■		■			■
Chionodoxa luciliae	■				■			■				■				■			■				
Choisya ternata	■	■					■		■						■	■						■	■
Chrysanthemum species		■	■		■			■					■	■	■	■	■	■		■			
Cineraria cruenta	■			■		■			■			■	■			■		■	■	■			
Citrus mitis	■	■	■	■	■				■					■		■					■		■
Clematis species		■	■		■					■					■	■	■	■	■				
Cobaea scandens		■	■		■					■					■				■				
Coleus blumei		■				■		■					■							■		■	
Convolvulus tricolor		■			■				■				■						■	■			
Cordyline species	■	■			■			■							■							■	
Cotoneaster species	■	■					■		■						■	■					■		
Crocus species	■			■	■			■				■				■	■		■				
Cyclamen species	■		■	■		■		■				■				■		■				■	
Cytisus × racemosus	■	■			■				■						■		■						■
Dahlia × cultorum		■	■		■			■					■	■	■	■	■	■	■	■			
Dianthus species		■			■				■			■	■			■		■		■			■
Eccremocarpus scaber		■	■		■					■					■		■	■					
Elaeagnus pungens	■	■					■		■						■						■	■	

	SEASON				POSITION			HABIT				HEIGHT				FLOWER COLOUR					OTHER FEATURES		
	Spring	Summer	Autumn	Winter	Sun	Shade	Any	Upright	Bushy	Climbing	Trailing/Spreading	Under 9in (22cm)	9-18in (22-45cm)	18in-3ft (45-90cm)	Over 3ft (90cm)	White/Cream	Yellow/Orange	Pink/Red	Blue/Purple	Multicoloured	Berries/Fruits	Attractive Foliage	Scent
Erica species	■	■	■	■	■				■			■				■		■	■			■	
Erysimum species	■			■	■				■				■				■	■					■
Euonymus species		■	■		■	■			■					■	■						■	■	
Fatsia japonica			■			■			■						■	■						■	
Forsythia species	■				■				■						■		■						
Fuchsia species		■	■		■	■			■		■		■	■		■		■	■	■			
Galanthus nivalis	■			■	■	■						■				■							
Gazania × *hybrida*		■	■		■				■			■					■	■		■			
Godetia grandiflora		■	■		■				■				■			■		■					
Gypsophila elegans		■	■		■				■				■			■		■					
Hebe species		■	■		■				■				■	■		■		■	■			■	
Hedera species				■	■	■				■	■				■						■	■	
Helianthemum alpestre	■	■			■						■	■				■	■	■					
Helichrysum petiolatum		■	■		■						■		■									■	
Heliotropium × *hybridum*		■	■		■				■				■						■				■
Hibiscus species		■	■		■				■						■	■		■	■				
Hosta species		■				■			■				■	■		■			■			■	
Humulus lupulus 'Aureus'		■	■		■	■				■					■							■	
Hyacinthus orientalis	■				■			■				■				■		■	■				■
Hydrangea species		■	■		■	■			■						■	■		■	■				
Iberis umbellata		■	■		■				■			■				■		■	■				
Ilex species			■	■	■	■		■							■						■	■	
Impatiens wallerana		■	■			■			■			■	■			■		■		■			
Ipomoea species		■	■		■					■					■	■		■	■				
Jasminum species	■	■	■	■	■	■				■					■	■	■						■
Juniperus species				■	■	■		■	■		■	■		■	■						■	■	
Kochia scoparia trichophylla		■	■		■			■						■								■	
Laburnum species	■	■			■										■		■						■
Lathyrus species		■	■		■					■					■	■		■	■				■
Laurus nobilis	■				■	■		■							■							■	
Lavandula angustifolia		■	■		■				■				■						■			■	■
Lilium species		■	■		■	■		■						■	■	■	■	■		■			■
Lobelia erinus		■	■		■	■					■	■				■		■	■				
Lonicera species		■	■		■	■				■					■	■	■	■			■		■
Lysimachia nummularia		■	■		■	■					■	■					■					■	
Magnolia species	■	■			■				■						■	■		■					■
Matthiola incana		■	■		■			■					■			■		■	■				■
Mesembryanthemum criniflorum		■	■		■						■	■				■	■	■		■			
Mimulus species		■	■			■			■			■	■				■	■		■			
Muscari species	■				■			■				■							■				■
Myosotis sylvatica	■				■	■			■			■				■		■	■				
Narcissus species	■			■	■	■		■				■	■			■	■			■			■
Nemesia strumosa		■			■				■			■				■	■	■	■	■			

	SEASON				POSITION			HABIT				HEIGHT				FLOWER COLOUR					OTHER FEATURES		
	Spring	Summer	Autumn	Winter	Sun	Shade	Any	Upright	Bushy	Climbing	Trailing/Spreading	Under 9in(22cm)	9–18in(22–45cm)	18in–3ft(45–90cm)	Over 3ft(90cm)	White/Cream	Yellow/Orange	Pink/Red	Blue/Purple	Multicoloured	Berries/Fruits	Attractive Foliage	Scent
Nepeta species	■	■	■				■		■				■						■			■	
Nerine bowdenii			■		■			■						■				■					
Nerium oleander		■	■		■				■						■	■		■					■
Nicotiana species		■	■				■	■						■		■		■					■
Oenothera missouriensis		■	■		■						■		■				■						
Olearia × haastii		■			■				■						■	■						■	
Paeonia lactiflora		■					■		■					■		■		■					■
Parthenocissus species			■				■			■					■							■	
Passiflora species		■	■		■					■					■	■			■		■		
Pelargonium hybrids		■	■		■				■		■		■			■		■				■	
Pernettya mucronata			■	■			■		■				■			■		■			■		
Petunia × hybrida		■	■		■				■		■		■			■		■	■	■			
Phormium tenax	■				■			■							■			■				■	
Plumbago capensis		■	■		■					■					■				■				
Polygonum baldschuanicum		■	■				■			■					■	■		■					
Primula species	■						■		■			■	■			■	■	■	■	■			■
Prunus species	■				■				■						■	■		■			■	■	■
Pyracantha species		■	■				■		■						■	■					■		
Reseda odorata		■	■		■				■				■				■						■
Rhododendron (azaleas)	■					■			■					■		■	■	■		■			■
Rosa species		■	■		■				■	■				■	■	■	■	■		■			■
Rosmarinus officinalis	■	■			■				■					■					■			■	■
Salpiglossis sinuata		■	■		■			■						■			■	■	■	■			
Salvia species		■	■		■				■				■	■				■	■				
Saxifraga species	■	■					■				■	■				■	■	■				■	
Schizanthus pinnatus		■			■			■						■		■		■	■	■			
Scilla species	■						■	■				■				■		■	■				
Sedum species		■	■		■						■	■				■	■	■				■	
Sempervivum species		■			■						■	■					■	■				■	
Senecio cineraria	■	■			■				■					■			■					■	
Skimmia japonica	■			■			■		■					■		■		■			■	■	■
Solanum species		■	■		■					■					■	■			■		■		
Stachys lanata		■			■						■		■					■				■	
Tagetes species		■	■		■				■				■				■	■		■			
Thunbergia species	■	■			■					■					■	■	■						
Tropaeolum species		■	■		■					■	■		■				■	■		■			
Tulipa hybrids	■						■	■					■	■		■	■	■		■			
Verbena species		■	■		■						■		■			■		■	■	■			
Viola × wittrockiana	■	■	■	■			■		■			■				■	■	■	■	■			
Vitis species			■				■			■					■						■	■	
Wisteria species	■	■			■					■					■	■		■	■				■

INDEX

Picture credits

Robin Bath: 16L. Elly Beintema/Vision International: 19, 34, 80. Michael Boys: 82R, 103, 110L. Michael Boys/Susan Griggs Agency: 36, 91, 111. David Bradfield: 25, 46, 48, 78. Pat Brindley: 38, 73, 99T. Richard Bryant/Arcaid: 59. Guy Burgess: 42. Linda Burgess: 9, 30, 33, 50, 70, 104, 105R, 106. Mike Burgess: 97, 99B. Eric Crichton: 35TL, 52R, 83. Melchior Digiacomo/The Image Bank: 14. EWA/Spike Powell: 92. EWA/Tim Street-Porter: 109. EWA/Jerry Tubby: 82L. Derek Fell: 87. Femina/Camera Press: 76. Valerie Finnis: 66, 77B. Robin Forbes/The Image Bank: 53. John Garrett: 40, 89. Robert Harding Picture Library/D & S Cavanaugh: 71. Iris Hardwick Library of Photographs: 68. Jerry Harpur: 47L, 47R. John Heseltine: 6. Hoyer/Snowdon/Vision International: 26. Impact Photos/Pamla Toler: 58B, 74. Monique Jacot/Susan Griggs Agency: 62. Leslie Johns: 93T, 93B. Paolo Koch/Vision International: 52L. Lucinda Lambton/Arcaid: 61. Christopher Lloyd: 20. Tania Midgley: 10L, 11, 13, 17, 22, 23R, 29, 41, 54, 57, 64T, 64B, 65, 98. Horst Munzig/Susan Griggs Agency: 35R. Bradley Olman/Bruce Coleman Inc: 108. Harry Smith: 28L, 44, 84, 95. Jessica Strang: 58T, 86L, 100. Michael Warren, A.B.I.P.P.: 77T.